TRAUMA and the
STRUGGLE TO OPEN UP

TRAUMA and the STRUGGLE TO OPEN UP

From Avoidance to
Recovery and Growth

Robert T. Muller

W. W. Norton & Company
Independent Publishers Since 1923
New York • London

For information about permission to reproduce selections from this book, write to Permissions, W. W. Norton & Company, Inc., 500 Fifth Avenue, New York, NY 10110

For information about special discounts for bulk purchases, please contact W. W. Norton Special Sales at specialsales@wwnorton.com or 800-233-4830

Manufacturing by LSC Harrisonburg
Production manager: Christine Critelli

Library of Congress Cataloging-in-Publication Data

Names: Muller, Robert T., author.
Title: Trauma and the struggle to open up : from avoidance to
recovery and growth/ Robert T. Muller.
Description: First edition. | New York : W.W. Norton & Company, [2018] |
Series: A Norton professional book | Includes bibliographical references.
Identifiers: LCCN 2017060909 | ISBN 9780393712261 (hardcover)
Subjects: LCSH: Psychic trauma—Treatment. | Psychotherapist and patient. | Psychotherapy.
Classification: LCC RC552.P67 M86 2018 | DDC 616.85/210651—dc23
LC record available at https://lccn.loc.gov/2017060909

W. W. Norton & Company, Inc., 500 Fifth Avenue, New York, N.Y. 10110
www.wwnorton.com

W. W. Norton & Company Ltd., 15 Carlisle Street, London W1D 3BS

1 2 3 4 5 6 7 8 9 0

To my parents,

Eva and Louis Muller.

With love.

Contents

Acknowledgments

Almost fifteen years ago, one of my colleagues, Catherine Classen, introduced me to a group of trauma therapists whose commitment to creative scholarship in the field was matched only by a deep commitment to the well-being of their clients. The International Society for the Study of Trauma and Dissociation would soon become my go-to place for clinical insight, support, and collaboration. I thank the society for providing a context for education and training in the field, excellence in research, and openness to novel interventions. Trauma therapy is hard to do without supportive colleagues.

My gratitude goes out to many people. The writing benefited greatly from comments, editorial changes, and critique provided by: Aviva Philipp-Muller, Mike Rand, Ruth Rohn, Steven Muller, and Diane Philipp. Daniel Lantos helped with early concept development; Aaron Philipp-Muller assisted with cultural memory content; Noah Philipp-Muller clarified linguistic details. Norton editors Ben Yarling and Deborah Malmud helped with earlier drafts of the manuscript.

Thanks also to my clinical site's monthly psychodynamic reading group. The opportunity to share clinical ideas, to challenge and learn from one another is priceless. Acknowledgment goes to Christie Hayos, Art Caspary, Diane Philipp, and Robyn Lam.

I am also grateful for the opportunity to teach and work with my doctoral and postdoctoral students, whose dedication to learning is unmatched: Sara Rependa, Leah Keating, Sheila Konanur, Kris Cordeiro, Laura Goldstein, Karina Zorzella, Julie Cinamon, and Kristin Thornback.

In addition, I would like to express my appreciation for my clients, who have been my best teachers.

Finally, this book could not have been written without the support and patience of my wife, friend, and colleague Diane Philipp, as well as my children, Aviva, Aaron, and Noah. Their love is nearly boundless. And that makes me very fortunate.

Introduction

We love, we hate, we fight, we fear. Our close relationships shape the contours of our lives.

They bring the greatest joy, they draw us into sadness. We fret we'll lose them . . . we lose them anyway. As children, they keep us alive. They bring the world color, they bring a lasting misery.

Our relationships sustain us, they help us endure. They bring a heavy pain, they challenge us. How we navigate them forms character. The feelings they stir dot the ups and downs of experience. They remind us of who we are, they dominate memory.

When they hurt, they consume us. When they don't, we take them for granted. They inform our coupling, our parenting.

They chapter the stories that make up our lives.

———

In a candid interview from a few years ago, renowned baseball pitcher and trauma survivor R. A. Dickey spoke to Canada's *National Post* (Fowles, 2013). He shared his perspectives on books, baseball, and what it means to heal from childhood sexual abuse. In Dickey's words:

Ultimately, the thing that helped me find some healing [was when] I learned that life was not about turning the page, or getting to the other side of something. It's about holding what is broken about the world, and holding what is joyful about the world, and being able to take a step forward with both. This is living well in the moment. And that's what I've tried to make a discipline of.

Relationships are at the center of human experience and at the heart of trauma. To hold the broken and the joyful, we must face the relationships that bring both. To heal from trauma is to embrace the truth of the past—the losses, the betrayals, the disappointments from those we trusted most.

This book is about trauma. It's about the relationships in our lives that hurt and harm. It's about the ones that help and heal.

Indeed when we study trauma, we see what a double-edged sword relationships are: Trauma stems *from* them. Recovery depends *on* them. The most harrowing trauma happens in close relationships, but recovery can't happen in isolation. Relationships are both poison *and* antidote. This, in part, is why we see the avoidance of closeness in many trauma survivors—a certain safety comes with avoidance, but the price is high.

I agree with R. A. Dickey: Healing doesn't come from turning the page. It comes from attending to the past and finding one's place in the here and now. It's not easy . . . even harder to do solo.

Opening up, facing our history, deliberately, authentically—this happens in the context of a healing relationship. How does this look, from beginning to end? How does a *shared telling* bring recovery and growth? How does trauma therapy *use* the relationship to heal? That is the subject of this book.

I get asked a lot, how did I develop an interest in trauma? I used to have a ready answer—one focusing on the intellectual side of me: my interest in research, clients, and so on. Perhaps true, in part. But a more honest answer was something I appreciated only in my early forties: My interest in trauma work stemmed from my past, my family's history.

My parents were school-age children during the Holocaust. They grew up in Budapest, Hungary. As Jews, their lives were, at the time, in constant danger. And they survived only because of a combination of luck and the goodwill of non-Jewish family members, who took great personal risks to help. As a young child, my mother was separated from her family, given false papers, and put into hiding with near-strangers—a sensible strategy, under the circumstances. With no family around for long stretches, she came terrifyingly close to having her identity revealed—some adults were keen to betray her as Jewish. It was only a fluke that she survived. As for my father, *his* father was killed. And after the war was over, my father—still a boy—learned a trade and went to work. He had to help support his family.

In my own consciousness—shaped by the stories told in my family—the legacy of the Holocaust was the *loss of childhood*. It's hard for me to imagine the terror my parents felt as children—terror so many others felt as well. The stories occupy a large space in my mind.

Families cope with trauma in different ways. Many share stories about the past. But many cope through silence, protecting themselves and loved ones from the truth. The truth can be unspeakable.

————

I use the term *trauma* throughout. What, in particular, am I referring to? This book focuses on the trauma that comes from relationships. These include disrupted early attachment, traumatic loss, maltreatment in the family, interpersonal abuse like domestic violence, and posttraumatic stress.[1] In each of these, an important trust has been broken. There are interpersonal losses or violations. Often, there's betrayal. And the effects are felt for years.

The treatment approach is *relational*, psychodynamic. It's grounded firmly in attachment theory, trauma theory, and the psychotherapy research that comes from both. It emphasizes the impact of family—both helpful and harmful—and the stories we come to live by. Since it's relational, it underscores the here and now, in the therapy office—the challenges and conflicts that happen in the treatment relationship.

With a relational approach, we focus a lot on how therapist and client affect each other. Sometimes, it's apparent how everything moves along well. Sometimes, the therapy falls off track. How the clinician *uses relationship difficulties* makes all the difference, and I'll look at how treatment might go better or worse, depending on choices the therapist makes.

1. Note that I will not be focusing on those traumatic experiences that come out of natural calamities, human-made disasters, traffic accidents, and the like.

The approach also encourages an honest, realistic stance toward experience, not blind optimism. Trauma *is* painful, it's a heavy load. There's no dressing that up. But it's a burden that can be understood, shared, made less scary, and, eventually, integrated. People who don't get help carry the burden their entire lives.

Pacing is a really important issue in this book, that is, the *pacing of therapy*. Like I say above, trauma is hard to deal with alone. When therapists help clients find a way to open up, to share the pain . . . that eases suffering. But how do we pace this? There are many horror stories of people feeling coerced into opening up. Revealing too much, too soon—it only makes the client feel worse. Then there are those who avoid their own past, sidestepping the trauma for years. For many, it's frightening to face, or it feels disloyal to talk badly of family. Or they've tried opening up, but nobody listened.

We know from research,[2] when people do address their trauma, they do much better. But *how* they open up, the pacing of it . . . how do we do this?

The key is in the relationship, the interpersonal stance the therapist takes with the client. This book walks through the relational approaches that help *pace the process of opening up*, so that clients find the experience helpful, not harmful.

Growth and development are also important themes here. It's clear that trauma therapy takes people down different paths. Of course, an important goal is recovery—we want people to feel better. But interpersonal trauma is complex. It touches people in different ways. It changes how they think about the world and their place in it. It shapes how they feel about family and friends, how they trust, how they love others, how they protect themselves.

As challenging as trauma treatment is, it can bring to people new understanding about themselves and others. How can trauma therapy facilitate growth and development? This is something we look at throughout, emphasizing the growth that comes from self-understanding, namely, greater appreciation for our competing emotional needs and awareness of the link between our traumatic past and our relational world.

Finally, throughout the book, I use case studies[3] to help illustrate the treat-

---

2. This research is described primarily in Chapters 1 and 4.

3. Throughout the book, when I refer to clients in a general sense, I use *they*, *he*, and *she* interchangeably. Case studies disguise all identifying information and are composites based on several actual clients.

ment process. In a field as emotionally charged as trauma, clients and therapists affect each other. For both, painful feelings get provoked. I use cases to explore my own experience with clients, my feelings toward them, and the feelings they express toward me. The cases include the ones that went well, as well as the ones where I struggled. And I'll talk about my therapeutic mistakes. Perhaps that's where we learn the most.

TRAUMA and the STRUGGLE TO OPEN UP

CHAPTER 1

When the Story Is Too Painful to Tell

A Telling

Years back, I had a psychotherapy client who would say almost nothing to me.

It's a strange feeling, sitting week after week alongside someone who speaks so little. Gaunt cheeks, pale skin, worryingly thin—when I began working with Maggie several weeks earlier, it was her family doctor who gave me much of the background story. During a physical exam, Maggie had refused a routine pap smear. An explanation on the risks of cervical cancer made no difference—she would have none of it. Her doctor assessed her for symptoms of mood disorder, started her on antidepressants, and decided to refer Maggie to me, suspecting a history of early abuse.

In our very first session, when asked about her background, Maggie confirmed those suspicions. Her older brother had repeatedly molested her, she explained flatly, elaborating on a couple of issues—mostly related to her eating disorder—and then promptly shut down for the next few weeks.

Excruciating is the word that comes to mind. Therapy sessions were cumbersome, painful, clumsy. I felt *deskilled*, as my colleagues in the field of trauma say. With her purse resting on her lap, Maggie would often shake agitatedly or stare numbly at a corner of the room. I found myself starting her sessions with a feeling of dread. And on those rare occasions when she would cancel the appointment, I would secretly feel relieved.

I gave up on asking her questions altogether, and often we just sat in silence. She was an enigma: nearly wordless, yet reliably taking time off from her responsibilities to come in for treatment, always punctual. And when I had to reschedule an appointment because of a conference, she confessed to feeling apprehensive, scared I wouldn't return.

I received Maggie's first e-mail to me as I walked back to my car after one of my daughter's theater performances. I found myself opening the message on my cell phone and scrolling to the top, in near disbelief that I'd received this communication at all. It was to be the first in a series of such contacts from her.

I read the top line: *I have something to tell you.* And she did just that, detailing a disturbing history of sexual abuse from a brother who'd been cruel and unpredictable.

Simply Telling

In the sessions that followed, not much changed, because in therapy change comes more slowly. And trauma therapy, in particular, takes time. *Simply telling*—relaying the details of a hurtful past in a torrent of words—doesn't bring relief on its own.

Psychiatrist Judith Herman wrote about this in her seminal work, *Trauma and Recovery* (1992):

> Patients at times insist upon plunging into graphic, detailed descriptions of their traumatic experiences, in the belief that simply pouring out the story will solve all their problems. . . . The patient's desire for this kind of quick and magical cure is fueled by images of early, cathartic treatments of traumatic syndromes which by now pervade popular culture, as well as by the much older religious metaphor of exorcism. (p. 172)

The notion that, on its own, catharsis brings about healing—this isn't how change actually happens in psychotherapy. When clients rush to share details of their trauma stories, my concern is how they'll feel afterward, in the time between therapy sessions. On the way home, as they think about the meeting, will they find themselves feeling ashamed? In fact, much later in our work together, I came to understand just how silent Maggie had always been about the abuse, believing she had no alternative, never having talked about specifics, until the e-mail she sent me.

Yet the wish to unload is understandable—finally, someone lending a sympathetic ear, perhaps for the first time . . . it's tempting to share. But opening up too quickly, before feeling ready, can lead to a sense of being exposed, humiliated, vulnerable.

If unloading or simply telling isn't enough, if, indeed, it can make people feel worse for a while, then what kind of telling helps?

An honest, but safe telling—one that makes it possible to confront a cruel past, to share the burden with caring others, and in doing so makes traumatic memories, feelings, and losses more bearable. A telling that helps you face the emotional experiences and vulnerabilities from that past. A telling that brings about learning and growth, even if the process is a painful one. This is what's meant by *opening up*, what we'll be exploring.

Maggie's e-mails kept coming. And while the next few sessions were still painfully awkward, indeed virtually silent, something had shifted. We'd found a way to connect, and it would work this way, at least for a time. She would send me messages by e-mail, sometimes focusing on parenting her young son, sometimes focusing on her eating disorder. And then she would quietly sit with me in my office, when we met, until she was able to go further.

An Honest Telling

Psychotherapist Rachel Sopher also found it hard to speak when she started treatment. A grandchild of a Holocaust survivor, Sopher recounts her family's story in a moving 2015 *New York Times* piece titled "Our Secret Auschwitz." Referring to the silence of her childhood home as a heavy pall, she came to discover only at the age of twelve that her grandfather had been imprisoned in Auschwitz. Prior to that, the story had been kept from her. Guarding this secret, evading the truth, had become her family's way of coping with a dreadful past. In her words:

We were trapped in history and did not understand how or why. Confusing things happened without explanation. We didn't celebrate birthdays, anniversaries, graduations. We somehow knew not to try to get close. Intimacy was painful because you never knew when someone you loved would be taken away. The pact of secrecy kept us safe from the horror of the past, but it also kept us from moving on. (Sopher, 2015)

When her own psychotherapist, who was normally on the quieter side, explicitly labeled the Holocaust as a trauma—one that affected every life it touched—Sopher began to recognize its influence on her. Instead of sugarcoating the truth, her therapist answered with an honest *yes* when Sopher asked her big burning question: *Do you really think the trauma of the Holocaust impacted my family, impacted my life?*

Psychotherapy is a *telling*, a sharing of a very personal nature, within a safe and secure context. But some things are hard to talk about. And reaching a place where you can tell your painful trauma story with honesty and openness can take time. There are truths that are enormously difficult to face. Still, recovery from trauma means, at some point, becoming honest about the past. With help, Sopher became able to tell her story truthfully. She became proficient in the art of truth-telling. It could only become so because her therapist was willing to call it like it is, and because Sopher herself became genuinely curious about her family's past, about her own history.

The idea that psychotherapy requires honesty and openness shouldn't come as a surprise to anyone. But as Sopher's example shows us, telling a traumatic story honestly is, in fact, a lot harder than it seems.

A psychological assessment procedure, known as the Adult Attachment Interview (AAI), illustrates this point (George, Kaplan, & Main, 1996; Hesse, 1999; Steele & Steele, 2008). Based on the work of British psychiatrist John Bowlby, the potentially stressful interview focuses on early history and memory for personal life events, especially early relationships. The questions orient the person to think about instances when they were in need: At those times, how did their caregivers respond? When ill, or at times of separation or loss, or when they wanted comfort or emotional support, or when they were frightened? By assessing their responses to these questions, we can see the person's understanding of *attachment*, how they think about the world of relationships, the way interpersonal needs are (or aren't) met.

Central to this technique is that the technical stories, the actual facts, are far less important than the way the person *makes sense* of those facts. The individual's *state of mind* regarding their relational world is what matters here. Does the client become overwhelmed by emotion, as he tells of his "mother who selfishly isolated herself" after her husband died? If so, maybe the person is still consumed by his anger at Mom. Or, given the same set of life events, does the individual put his mother on a pedestal, perhaps casting her as a martyr, a victim whose husband unexpectedly died, leaving her alone and isolated? Same event, different interpretation. Or maybe, the story is told with a focus entirely on the father's death, a terrible event the client hasn't yet recovered from.

When working with families in therapy, we often see that siblings from the same home describe events in very different ways. Even when there's general agreement on basic facts, there are disagreements around the *meaning given* to those facts. And in the end, their stories seem unrecognizable from one another.

But an honestly told story is one that has balance. People who are classified as *securely attached* are balanced and flexible regarding relationships. They can look at themselves and their own interpersonal history honestly, even when painful to do so. They can see the story from different angles; they don't shut down. Using the example from just above, when the interviewee was asked whether he'd ever felt rejected as a child (a question from the AAI), this is the story he told:

Did I ever feel rejected as a child? Hmm . . . (pause for five seconds). Well, I kinda feel bad saying this, but I guess so. I mean, not that my mom did it on purpose. She got sort of depressed after our dad died. We all did a bit, I think. She hardly spoke any English, and couldn't find work, and the construction company my dad was working for refused to pay out his pension. I remember one time my sister was in the washroom. And my sister . . . I guess she got her period. She was younger than me, and I felt kinda responsible for her. But I would've felt dumb going into the washroom to help her—I was fourteen so it would've been weird. So, I knocked on my mom's bedroom door for help, and . . . she was drunk again, and . . . (eyes well up with tears) and . . . she did *nothing*, no help, told me to go figure it out myself, and she just stayed in her room . . . she did nothing. My sister was crying, she was scared, didn't know what was going on . . . I, I guess as I think about it now, I did feel rejected, and hurt, it's true . . . as if we just didn't matter all that much. And I felt bad for my sister, she was just so *scared* and everything. I couldn't help her. I mean, I've done okay, but uh . . . she's still got tons of problems. So . . . there you go (pause). Whoo! (deep sigh) I wasn't expecting to tell you about all that!

In this version of the same set of events, this young man, still pained by his past, would be classified as securely attached. Why?

The hallmark of secure attachment is balance. Reflecting on events that were emotionally disturbing, does the person do so with balance? Here, yes. When asked whether he'd ever felt rejected as a child, he tells how his mother's incapacitation left her unable to help, how she was unresponsive to his calls for assistance. And in recounting these earlier life events, he's hurt, he feels pained, yet he also has empathy. He's neither so overwhelmed by his feelings that he's stopped from telling the painful story, nor is he minimizing it, or putting a positive spin on it, by perhaps telling it as an example of how cleverly he helped his sister in the end.

His telling is honest, it rings true. The emotions are consistent with the remembered events. The speaker neither defends Mom as some kind of martyr nor vilifies her without reason. He lives in a world where relationships matter, and his mother's failure to be there for him and his sister—when they needed her most—deeply hurt. Told like this, the story adds up. Still, hearing this account, one might worry for him, whether in intimate relationships he'll show signs of what Bowlby called *compulsive caregiving*. Will he try to take care of others to make up for earlier losses and hurts?

In this example, the young man would be categorized as *earned secure*, a version of secure attachment in which the person has suffered much adversity but has found a flexible way to make sense of those events, an attribute necessary for resilience. The sudden death of his father, and his mother's later depression had a big impact on him. And yet, there is in him a certain maturity, an ability to step back and share his story with authenticity.

Some people can manage this, but for most, this is a very tall order.

Secure Attachment—Rare in Trauma Survivors

As I said above, telling a traumatic story with honesty and openness is a lot harder than it seems. Among trauma survivors, secure attachment is more the exception than the rule.

Studies that have recorded different attachment patterns among people with high-risk histories show that relatively few trauma survivors are securely attached. And few are able to tell their story, to talk about their distressing past without great difficulty.

My colleague, psychologist Catherine Classen, and I have looked at this very issue in a clinical research initiative at Women's College Hospital in Toronto, Ontario. The Women Recovering from Abuse Program (Duarte Giles et al., 2007) is an eight-week group therapy model that focuses on safety and stabilization skills. It takes place over four half-days each week and uses a continuous enrollment process, so that every week one or two women start treatment while one or two group members complete the program. Before they received therapy, we conducted extensive testing, looking at the attachment patterns of a group of these women, all of whom had profound histories of interpersonal trauma and were psychologically symptomatic (for example, depression, anxiety, relationship problems). Using well-trained and reliable coders who were experienced in attachment classification, we found that only 8 percent of these very high-risk women were rated as having a secure attachment orientation (Classen, Muller, Field, Clark, & Stern, 2017; Classen, Zozella, Keating, Ross, & Muller, 2016).[1]

And our results aren't unusual, compared to the work others are doing in the field. A study funded by the National Institute of Mental Health also investigated highly symptomatic women, with histories of childhood physical or sexual abuse, and found similarly low levels of secure attachment (about 17 percent), especially among the ones who showed symptoms of posttraumatic stress disorder (PTSD) from their early abuse (Stovall-McClough & Cloitre, 2006).

Studies that have recorded attachment patterns among those with very high-risk histories haven't only looked at treatment-seeking, psychologically symptomatic people. This is important, because one might argue that, by virtue of being in psychological distress—symptomatic and seeking psychotherapy—these people might appear insecure in their interpersonal relationships. When trauma survivors aren't in psychological distress, when they aren't symptomatic and seeking treatment, do they fare better in terms of their attachment patterns? We certainly know of such people. What does research say about those who have suffered a terrible past, but who are simply progressing routinely with their lives, out in the community? How do they compare regarding their attachment orientation?

---

1. See also Muller and Rosenkranz (2009).

Similarly to the treatment-seeking group, it turns out. As before, only a minority are securely attached. My students and I discovered this when I was working at the University of Massachusetts in Boston. In a study we conducted locally, we screened female and male adults and confirmed a history of childhood physical or sexual abuse among a subset of individuals—these were community members who were neither treatment-seeking nor clinically symptomatic. They were mostly working-class people, willing to give a half-day of their time, for nominal reimbursement.

What we found was very similar to the findings above. Among people with high-risk histories of trauma, about 24 percent were scored as secure in their attachment patterns (Muller, Lemieux, & Sicoli, 2001; Muller, Sicoli, & Lemieux, 2000; Muller, Kraftcheck, & McLewin, 2004). That means three-quarters were *not* secure. And these findings were virtually identical to those reported independently by psychologist Robin Lewis and colleagues working in Virginia (Lewis, Griffin, Winstead, Morrow, & Schubert, 2003). Few trauma survivors were classified as securely attached. If you compare these findings to other studies, *low-risk*[2] adults are far more likely to be classified as securely attached, at levels around 58 percent (Bakermans-Kranenburg & van IJzendoorn, 2009). In other words, trauma puts people at greater risk for insecure attachment.

So it seems that, whether adult trauma survivors are psychologically distressed and treatment seeking or not, among people with early histories of interpersonal trauma only a minority show the secure attachment pattern.

From this we learn just how unforgiving relational trauma can be. When we've experienced a cruel past, we're left insecure in our interpersonal world. Relationships, sex, closeness, parenting . . . are all profoundly affected. And the way we think about and understand our relationship history is affected as well.

Indeed, the very ability to talk about our past in a balanced way, to be honest and open about times when we experienced traumatic loss, hurt, or fear—the ability to freely reflect on such moments and how they've influenced our interpersonal lives—is greatly hindered.

And it's very hard to cope with something, when that something can't even be talked about.

---

2. By *low-risk*, I mean people from community samples not selected for any clinical disorder or history of trauma. See Bakermans-Kranenburg and van IJzendoorn (2009).

When the Expectation Is to Stay Silent

So telling a traumatic story honestly and openly is a lot harder than it seems. But all this leads to the question: Why tell at all?

Because, in the long run, holding it in doesn't work. In the next few chapters, we'll take a detailed look at the coping strategy of avoidance, how it appears in practice, and why people engage in it altogether. But for the moment, let's consider an example of what telling might look like in families where the expectation is to hold in thoughts and feelings surrounding interpersonal trauma.

In such homes, the script is to *pretend*, to shut down trauma-related feelings. Rigidity and defensiveness dominate over honesty and openness. And it can be very difficult when one family member has a different way of seeing the past, a way that doesn't mesh well with the view held by the rest. That person is often cast as a troublemaker.

In my clinical work, I've had families come see me when trauma incidents were recently revealed. And often, the one who insists on "rocking the boat" is scapegoated by others in the family, leaving that person feeling alone and isolated, as though the insistence on speaking the truth somehow makes them crazy.

There can be a family expectation to minimize interpersonal trauma, to stay silent. In "One Million Tiny Plays about Britain" (2008), playwright Craig Taylor depicts the rift that arises between family members as he walks us through a tortured conversation between mother and son in the wake of family trauma.

The setting is a Manchester hospital room, where Alex, a young adult, is a patient. His mother is by his bedside. One after another, mother shows Alex all the get well cards he's received, reading aloud everyone's upbeat messages. Unquestionably earnest, the mother wants nothing more than for her son to *be happy*. She tells him how flowers would make the hospital room less dark, that winter doesn't last forever, and how supportive everyone has been. The cards Alex received are filled with platitudes: "Think sunny thoughts," and "Turn that frown upside down."

Soon, we come to understand how Alex ended up in the hospital, as his mother innocently asks him about his hand. He answers her with cold irritation, "It's my wrist. It's not my hand." And with that, we realize the truth: He'd tried to slit his wrists, he'd tried to kill himself.

And how does his mother cope with the truth, with the near-loss of her son?

"I thought it best to keep it in the family," she says, suggesting a pattern of secrecy, of cover-up, later dismissing the contents of his suicide note as something he couldn't possibly have meant. Tragically, the attempt to make her son feel better, to "fix" him, makes him feel worse. Soon she gives him another get well card, this one from his sister—a drawing of a man with a big chin.

The caption reads, "Chin up!"

As painful discussion is shut down, what Alex doesn't receive is a much-needed sense of validation. His family is ill-equipped. In the aftermath of such crises, in many such families, there's an attempt to sweep the secret under the rug, forgetting about it, pretending it never happened at all.

To tell one's painful story but to have it dismissed or minimized can become an exercise in frustration and retraumatization. In this way, even an honest telling that falls on deaf ears is doomed.

A Shared Telling

Let's think back to Rachel Sopher's story from earlier in the chapter. Recall that her family had silenced the truth for decades. To not know that her own grandfather had gone through the Holocaust and that he'd spent part of his life in a chronic state of terror meant not knowing her family at all. Recall also that, over time, Sopher came to recognize the truth of her family's past because she became interested in her own history, wishing to have it covered up no more.

But equally important, Sopher was fortunate enough to have someone to help her through it all. It would be impossible to overstate the helpfulness of interpersonal support in the aftermath of trauma, to have someone share in the experience.

In his work exploring PTSD recovery in combat veterans, war correspondent Sebastian Junger (2016) showed how, in societies with high levels of interpersonal support, PTSD rates tend to be quite low. This is seen when combatants return from a tour of duty and feel a sense of acceptance rather than alienation.

In Junger's view, being part of a *tribe*—to help you through—can make all the difference. And from his own personal experience of living in New York City in the wake of the 9/11 attacks on the World Trade Center, Junger observed a dramatic—albeit temporary—increase in interpersonal support in the community. He described this in a Canadian Broadcasting Corporation interview in May of 2016, explaining that people came together in a way they hadn't before—they felt needed by others.

Recovery from trauma is hard to do alone. As I said before, psychotherapy is a telling, a personal sharing . . . the relational aspect of psychotherapy is central to healing.

Psychotherapists from different schools of thought—who tend to disagree on a lot—still agree that the connection between clinician and client can make or break treatment. Different reasons are given for this. Therapists from the cognitive-behavioral school tend to view good rapport and collaboration as necessary for treatment strategies to be accepted by the client (Perris, 2000). That is, a good psychotherapy relationship makes it easier for clients to take in new learning and skills. In contrast, more experiential, psychodynamic therapists tend to emphasize the therapy relationship as curative in its own right—a good relationship heals.

Experience tells me both are true. In my first treatment book, *Trauma and the Avoidant Client* (Muller, 2010), I said that the therapist-client relationship is central to good outcome in psychotherapy. And research in the field supports this idea.

A statistical technique known as meta-analysis has had a great impact on health and mental health research, and psychotherapy research in particular. Originally developed independently by statisticians Gene Glass, who worked in educational psychology, and John Hunter, who studied personnel selection, the technique is used to gather findings across studies. This proved to be especially important in the area of psychotherapy outcome research because, over the years, there have been so many different kinds of psychotherapy, with widely differing claims regarding its benefits. It was critical to see if such claims had merit.

Glass copublished the first meta-analysis on the benefits of psychotherapy in the late 1970s (Smith & Glass, 1977; Smith, Glass, & Miller, 1980), but among the most exhaustive works on the topic is psychologist Bruce Wampold's *The Great Psychotherapy Debate* (2001). Summarizing the many meta-analyses that have looked at psychotherapy outcome, Wampold found that relationship factors such as the alliance between clinician and client were much more important in a successful treatment than anything else the therapist had control over. And these findings have been corroborated repeatedly. A good therapy relationship, where there's empathy, warmth, acceptance, and encouragement, was found to be much more helpful than the specific school of thought the clinician used.

Nowhere is the therapeutic relationship more valuable than in recovery from interpersonal trauma. The opportunity to share with someone who is nonjudgmental, who takes one's story seriously, who listens without overreacting, and who can help find new perspectives . . . such an opportunity can be life-altering. In *Trauma and the Avoidant Client* (2010), I wrote:

> Clients who have experienced considerable rejection and hurt in their families of origin, rejection that has gone unacknowledged and unresolved, need a safe context within which they are given the opportunity to experience relationships in new ways. When safety and security characterize the therapeutic relationship, such interaction may represent the client's first occasion to experience support, encouragement, and emotional vulnerability with an empathic other. (p. 45)

A few years ago, some of my graduate students in the Trauma and Attachment Lab at York University became interested in studying the therapeutic relationship in trauma treatment. In partnership with several local community mental health agencies, we developed a project to look at this. How do clients and their therapists feel about each other, and their work together? We looked at children getting therapy for posttraumatic symptoms due to recent sexual abuse and other traumatic events (Konanur, Muller, Cinamon, Thornback, & Zorzella, 2015; Rependa & Muller, 2015; Zorzella, Muller, & Cribbie, 2015; Zorzella, Rependa, & Muller, 2017).

As part of their treatment, these children were invited to put together a trauma narrative. Developed by psychiatrist Judith Cohen and psychologists Anthony Mannarino and Esther Deblinger (Cohen, Mannarino, & Deblinger, 2006), this approach helps clients tell their trauma story, in written form, in collaboration with a clinician. Importantly, the therapist never disagrees with the client or makes suggestions on how remembered events unfolded. Rather, the clinician helps the person make *sense* of subjective experiences. For example, if this or that event is recalled, if the individual made this choice or that, fought back or didn't . . . what does it *mean* to them? What does the client worry it *says* about them, or about their future? And how can they start putting their feelings about themselves, and their traumatic story, into context?

The trauma narrative is really hard to do. And the therapists on our team were worried. After all, their clients were just kids—young girls and boys who'd been sexually abused. And here we were, inviting these vulnerable children to talk about very disturbing experiences. Previous research by Cohen and colleagues had shown this to be a promising approach, *as long as* safety and stabilization strategies—which we taught them—were established first (an important treatment component, to be discussed in later chapters).

Still, we wondered about the wisdom of what we were doing. Many tense discussions among members of the clinical and research teams led to the same questions: By encouraging children to *talk about* their traumatic experiences would we *retraumatize* them? And would they become so distressed that they would psychologically push their therapists away?

What we found was just the opposite. Children improved—no retraumatization. During the period of assessment and treatment, these high-risk children showed reductions in posttraumatic symptoms, which remained low even months after treatment ended (Konanur et al., 2015). This is what we were hoping for, and what prior research had shown, so we weren't exactly shocked (although we *were* relieved!).

But what was especially different here was our examination of the therapeutic relationship. Recall that these young, vulnerable children were invited to write about their painful traumatic experiences, and we didn't know what this would do to the working relationship between children and therapists. Their clinicians were supposed to be people kids would trust. By engaging in these trauma narratives, would children come to view their therapists negatively? Would they push them away?

Once again, on the contrary: when children were initially queried about their therapists and their work together, the kids rated clinicians highly. And over the course of treatment—even after the challenging trauma narrative—children's feelings about their therapists improved further. The evidence was clear: A collaborative sharing of traumatic experiences helped, rather than harmed, the therapeutic relationship. And when therapists and (nonabusive) parents were independently asked for *their* impressions as well, the responses were in line with those of the children (Rependa & Muller, 2015; Zorzella et al., 2017).

For these kids, sharing their traumatic stories with a caring other led to even greater feelings of closeness and collaboration with that person. And these increases all went along with reductions in posttraumatic symptoms, gains that were maintained long after treatment ended.

As in the personal story recounted by Rachel Sopher, these children benefited from having a partner to help them through a painful telling. Given the opportunity to share their burden, they no longer had to endure it alone. They were no longer silent.

A Growthful Telling

Sometimes our clients make changes in ways that are surprising—and quite rewarding. This was something I saw with Maggie, from earlier in this chapter.

Recall that Maggie's low weight, depression, and refusal to have a routine pelvic exam raised her family doctor's suspicions of prior sexual abuse, prompting the referral to me. I worked with Maggie in near silence for several weeks, often feeling frustrated and confused about whether this was helpful at all, yet recognizing that she was coming in regularly, and that she was as engaged as she could tolerate.

Other than a brief disclosure of early abuse, I was kept in the dark about much of her past, until she began e-mailing me strange disconnected facts on her frightening history as a child, at which point her backstory became a bit clearer. When she was about eight, her fourteen-year-old brother would seek her out and sexually exploit her, threatening her if she didn't keep quiet about it. That's about all I knew.

I started bringing to sessions a printed copy of any e-mails she would send me, plainly setting them down on the table between us, expressing little more than warm curiosity, but no pressure. And with the help of the deep breathing skills I'd taught her in earlier sessions, she soon began picking up the reams of printed material, thumbing through them, and eventually opening up.

We worked together for the next year and a half in active phase-based trauma treatment[3] (discussed in later chapters), first helping stabilize her dangerously low weight and mood. Some of these sessions included her husband, who was,

---

3. A phase-based approach applies trauma therapy in stages, with a focus first on feeling safe. Often clinicians employ techniques such as relaxation, grounding skills, psychoeducation, and emotion regulation. Next, there is direct experiencing and processing of trauma-related memories and feelings, with reflection on the meaning of these experiences in the person's life. Finally, there is reconnection with aspects of oneself, and with supportive interpersonal relationships. The approach is detailed in Chapter 4. See Cloitre et al. (2011).

to my relief, rather gentle both with her and with their seven-year-old son. In time, I invited her to tell me more about her early history, and eventually we put together a trauma narrative.

This was difficult for her to do, for good reason. She'd been a young, shy child, victimized for at least two years by her older, stronger male sibling. It was all very hard to talk about. By the time her brother was sixteen and found dead a few blocks from their apartment building (killed in a gang-related drug incident), he'd penetrated her numerous times with various objects and had once forced intercourse on her. Discussing her traumatic experiences, facing them, struggling with their implications was scary. She had no idea where the telling would lead. But she stuck with it.

Maggie shared her story with honesty. And for me, sitting with her as she did so, was challenging. She would become visibly anxious, sometimes reliving the particulars of her past. I would then talk her through her breathing, instructing her in grounding techniques, like rubbing her hands together and other sensory experiences, to remind her she was now safe. And then we would continue the process. As a child she'd felt terrified, betrayed, violated. But as we worked together, she reached a point where she could sit with vulnerable feelings alongside someone she could trust. She could increasingly face the truth of her traumatic story and what it meant to her, without becoming so overwhelmed.

And here's where the surprising part came in. I didn't know it yet, but in the therapeutic work that followed, I would come to see in Maggie a change I could not have anticipated: new learning that went beyond recovery, learning that came from the process of opening up, out of facing her traumatic history . . . but then went further. The word that describes it best is *growth*.

It's odd to think of growth in a context like this: development in the wake of painful loss. We're so used to equating trauma with tragedy.

Then again, the idea that something of value can come of adverse life experiences is really nothing new. Making lemonade of life's proverbial lemons—a lesson popularized by self-help guru and quintessential optimist Dale Carnegie—is based on a phrase penned at least a century ago. But what I'm referring to here is novel in important ways.

Posttraumatic growth, the notion that beneficial changes can come in the aftermath of traumatic events, *is* different. It's an important idea, but it's one that's easily misunderstood. It shouldn't be confused with sugarcoating, getting people to look at the "bright side" of their adversity. Reassuring people who have suffered profoundly that their past has a silver lining is, at best, naïve and, at worst, just plain thoughtless. I have on occasion supervised junior therapists excited about positive psychology, attempting to help clients see things less pessimistically, but too quick to find simple answers to painful questions. And from such well-intentioned interventions, clients end up feeling worse.

Jim Rendon, a journalist who recently conducted dozens of interviews with trauma therapists and clients, cautions: "Who wants to be told they should be growing when they are in so much pain they can't function? Making clients believe that they should be strong, even when they are in mental agony, can cause them to reject the idea of growth entirely and may even thwart their desire to continue with therapy" (2015, pp. 218–219).

I agree—people who have suffered need to know that their pain is taken seriously, that it's not minimized, that their therapist is actually paying attention.

And recognition of posttraumatic growth shouldn't be romanticizing adversity either, rationalizing trauma, as in, *It made me stronger.* In describing his dreadful one-year journey escaping from Afghanistan at age twelve with the help of human traffickers, author Gulwali Passarlay (2016) overcame enormous obstacles, risking his life many times, and finally making it to England. Along the way as a refugee, he was lied to, humiliated, beaten and imprisoned. He lived in constant fear of the unknown.

In a Canadian Broadcasting Corporation interview in January 2016, now a young man, he explained that despite all he'd achieved, learning life "the hard way" (in his words), he still wished the past could be undone, that he could have his family back. And he certainly didn't wish such harrowing experiences on *any* child, being sent to the unknown, having to risk one's life for safety.

Tales of overcoming adversity are always compelling, and it's easy to overlook the suffering by focusing on how, in the end, the protagonist experienced growth. But recognition of posttraumatic growth is not to dismiss, minimize, or romanticize suffering. Rather, it's to notice that traumatic experiences *do* change people, sometimes in surprising, even enriching ways. It's an idea that has gained traction in recent years, less about the changes that come of the traumatic event per se than about changes arising from the individual's struggle afterward, laboring to understand painful, life-altering experiences (Calhoun, Cann, & Tedeschi, 2010; Calhoun & Tedeschi, 1998).

In their extensive research on the topic, psychologists Richard Tedeschi and Lawrence Calhoun found that trauma survivors who report growth may very well have experienced considerable distress from traumatic events. It's not that they somehow lucked out, or evaded painful feelings or suffering; but that, eventually, these people also engaged in a process of active self-reflection and reevaluation.

In trauma, ideas about the world and how things ought to work—the illusions we operate under daily, to feel safe and secure—no longer fit our lived experiences. And this requires a reckoning. Survivors who involve themselves in this kind of reconstructive process are able to move beyond the trauma, to make a new life for themselves. In columnist David Brooks's words, "Having faced death, people in these circumstances are forced to confront the elemental questions of life" (Brooks, 2015).

And it's in that confrontation where the potential for growth lies. A *growthful telling* is effortful—an attempt to make sense of the trauma *and* the way it connects to one's overall life narrative. It's an exercise that can open new questions surrounding adaptation and change, who or what was lost, who or what is important in life. And, a growthful telling can lead to new learning, for example, gaining greater clarity on core values, inner strengths, and vulnerabilities.

In the telling of important life stories we always engage in selective remembering. Narrative psychotherapy innovator Michael White said that we prune from our lived experiences those events that don't fit with the dominant narrative, and that much of our experience is never told or expressed—it remains without organization or shape (White & Epston, 1990). This happens a lot with traumatic events, where memories crystalize alongside dominant themes like, *You can't rely on anyone.*

But rarely do we examine or question ourselves and our understanding. As we tell our trauma story anew, are there more subtle lessons about ourselves that we'd never considered? As we reexamine our painful stories, are there *nondominant* narratives that never crossed our minds? Are there lessons that can be instructive, that open the door to new views of ourselves and our potential?

Tedeschi and Calhoun consider posttraumatic growth to be comparable to wisdom, writing that, "only an integrative perspective taken by the wise can encompass these paradoxes of trauma and growth" (Calhoun et al., 2010, p. 233).

Yes, a tall order . . . but it does happen. I started to see this with Maggie about four years into our work together.

By now she was much less symptomatic, feeling and looking better. Her weight was normal, she was no longer overexercising, and she had been taken off antidepressants at least a year earlier. A library assistant by training, who'd been on disability for several months prior to starting treatment, she was now working from time to time, in queue for a possible full-time position in the fall. She wasn't elusive anymore when referring to the trauma, or afraid to mention her brother's name, as if doing so would somehow conjure him from the dead. Rather, she would *notice* traumatic memories as they arose, owning them, feeling them . . . recognizing them as painful aspects of her past, but not letting them define or consume her.

But where I noticed posttraumatic growth especially was in her role as a mother. There were many examples of this, but I'll share a poignant one. On this occasion, she came in telling me of a parent-teacher meeting at her son's school, where things went badly. Now finishing the fifth grade, her child had been diagnosed previously with a learning disability. Based on some earlier concerns, I'd initiated a referral for him to undergo a learning assessment, which had helped her and her husband as parents. And for a while, they'd handled it all quite well, but during this one parent-teacher meeting, Maggie—in her words—"lost it" on the teacher.

The exact sequence of events was a bit unclear. But in her therapy session, what Maggie realized was that during the meeting with the teacher she'd been triggered. Mainly, she'd become convinced her son was being badly treated, that the school was denying him needed services. She lost composure, becoming frankly insulting with the teacher, making for a situation that was loud— and rather embarrassing for her low-key husband.

The conflict itself was resolved quickly, with the aid of the school principal. But in session, what bugged Maggie was her overreaction. What had gotten into her? She wanted to understand it better. And while many themes emerged over the next few weeks, an important one was that of *protection*.

Maggie reflected on the one time she told her mother about the abuse. She'd shared this story with me before, but as we reconsidered its meaning this time around, she made connections she hadn't thought of earlier. Her mother had responded to the shocking revelation with a kind of dismissiveness, one that turned to anger, denying outright that the abuse could be true. Wagging her finger at Maggie, she'd told her to take it back and promise never to speak of it again.[4]

4. How parents react when their children disclose traumatic experiences (such as sexual or physical abuse, bullying, or incest) has an enormous impact on child well-being and recovery afterward. Children fare much better when parents respond to the child without judgment or criticism. See Cinamon (2016).

At the time, Maggie felt utterly alone, vulnerable, betrayed. And now, the thought of being anything but protective of her own child—of being anything like her mother—terrified her.

Together, we worked to make sense of this simple school meeting that had triggered her so, thinking about her *identity* as a mother, still in formation, and her decision to set loyalty to her family as a priority—how the thought of making mistakes as a mother scared her, how she worried that her decisions could damage her child, but also how she wouldn't be able to protect him forever, or protect him from everything.

We also reflected on the hurtful impact she sometimes had on others. Her determination to protect her son led to actions *unlike* her mother's, but that same characteristic could lead to behavior *just like* her mother's (such as verbally abusing a young, unsuspecting teacher)—behavior she didn't like but recognized in herself. And how curious it all was, that she could so stridently stand up for her child yet still struggle to stand up for herself.

This took several weeks to unpack. As we would consider one issue, it would become clear just how many others there were to explore.

Maggie continued in therapy until the end of that summer. In the fall, she did, in fact, begin full-time work, so we shifted to occasional "maintenance" sessions. No longer haunted by her past, she could rely more on the people in her life—those she cared about and who cared about her—with greater openness came greater freedom. And with that, she needed me less.

———————

The next few chapters look at some of the things that stop clients from opening up, why opening up is easier said than done, how the therapeutic relationship is central to the process, and what it means, in practice, to face a cruel past.

CHAPTER 2

How Traumatized Clients Avoid the Past, Painful Feelings, and Relationships

The Case of Nicholas

The waiting room at my clinical site has two long sofas, a couple of simple armchairs, and some houseplants; the tall windows give it an airy feel. It's a common space shared by a half dozen or so therapists, occupying the third floor of the outpatient clinic where I practice. For a few minutes before their sessions, people with unrelated pasts find themselves sharing this normally quiet area. In an unplanned way, clients seeing therapists for different reasons find themselves interacting with one another, or trying not to.

On any given morning, a mother, waiting for her child's assessment to be done, may be seated across a young couple who've had yet another miscarriage, facing the anxious prospect of never having children at all. And perhaps, pacing at the far end of the waiting area—unable to bring himself to sit beside the young couple—is a gentleman whose wife was recently killed in a car accident, two years into what was going to be a great retirement.

By five or ten minutes past the hour, the room clears. All is silent, and soon the space fills anew. It was because of my client Nicholas that I first noticed the curious theater of my simple waiting area. One thing I almost never hear coming from there is laughter. But Nicholas could make people laugh—however briefly—somehow pulling together the disparate characters in the room, finding common topics to make light of. With his deep, booming voice, he'd make himself front and center. And for the client I'd see in the session before his, the chuckling from down the hall was initially distracting, and soon downright irritating.

Nicholas's sense of humor worked well for him. An ESL (English as a second language) instructor at a local community college, he was popular with his students. He rightly pointed out that, without exception, my waiting area plants were actually weeds, telling me they were virtually indestructible: I couldn't kill them if I *wanted* to. And although he liked to tease, he'd also find ways to poke fun at himself, which would somehow ease the sting.

At age forty-nine, Nicholas had never had a relationship longer than 6 months. To those close to him, he was at once endearing and insufferable. It was his girlfriend, Karina, a spiritual healer, who first contacted me about whether I worked with "commitment-phobes," as she succinctly put it. She loved him but found him impossible to "pin down." At age thirty-nine, she was now considering having children, and as she feared, the idea didn't go over well with Nicholas.

After a few ugly arguments, she gave him an ultimatum, threatening to end the relationship unless he went for psychotherapy. Soon, Nicholas contacted me directly (I'd explained to Karina that he would have to book appointments himself). And in the first session, he repeated what I already knew from her, about the arguments they'd been having. But he also told me about his recent panic attacks.

It seemed that a week or so after the ultimatum, as they were watching a romantic comedy at a movie theater, he found himself unable to breath, a frightening condition he sometimes struggled with. The symptoms escalated quickly, and he was afraid he would choke. This episode was so bad they had to leave.

On the steps of Karina's downtown apartment, Nicholas told her about his bad dreams. It had been a couple of years, but the recurring nightmares about his father were happening again. They were now so vivid, he was afraid to go to sleep.

It also seemed the nightmares were quite violent. And when I asked him to elaborate, he explained his father was "old school," from Greece. Knocking their kids around, now and then, was how *all* Greek dads got a good workout, he quipped. Wrapping up the topic, before changing the subject entirely, he added: *No reason to make a big deal of it.*

When Trauma Brings Self-Deception

Recall the Adult Attachment Interview (AAI), described in Chapter 1, how it assesses a person's understanding of attachment, their view on how interpersonal needs are met, and how they think about the world of relationships—the client's relational state of mind (George et al., 1996; Hesse, 1999; Steele & Steele, 2008). The approach orients interviewees to think about their early experiences with caregivers. Central to the procedure is that the technical stories, the actual facts, are far less important than how the person makes *sense* of those facts. How do they make meaning of their own story? How do they reflect on and feel about their early history? For example, what emotions come up as they describe their memory for events, and what feelings are conspicuously sidestepped? What portrait are they painting of themselves, and what image are they maintaining of important others? What are they unwilling to let go of, and what can they not bear to look at?

In the second meeting I had with Nicholas, we did the AAI. Early in the interview, the person is asked to list five adjectives describing their childhood relationship with a given caregiver, going back as far as they remember.

In describing his childhood relationship with his mother, the first adjective Nicholas listed was *good: She was a good mother.* After he gave his five adjectives, as typical in AAI administration, I asked him to go back through the adjectives one at a time. As I mentioned, the first adjective he listed was *good.* I asked him to describe any specific incidents or memories that illustrated the relationship as good. Tell me about something that was good. As required in the AAI, I gave him no coaching, no clues, no examples of what "good" might look like. I let the chips fall where they may. This is what Nicholas said:

Well . . . my mother tried to abort me. Oh, the story is actually cute and funny. You see, she and I became very good friends later on. My mom said to me, "I used to jump up and down trying to get *rid* of you." Well, I just thought that was *really* funny. Can't you just picture that? . . . Her pregnant and jumping up and down?!

As Nicholas recalled this brief story, especially as he reached the last part about his pregnant mother jumping up and down, what struck me was how he was laughing.

Putting his whole body into it, he grinned as he bobbed his head and shoulders, illustrating the absurdity of what his mother had tried to do, to abort him. In fact, throughout our work, Nicholas would poke fun at his immigrant parents a lot, how their never having gone to university made for superstitious beliefs, for unschooled attitudes about health. Hence, wasn't it funny that his immigrant mother had tried to abort him, by jumping up and down?

Was it funny?

Like a lot of what we understand in mental health, the answer depends on context. Depending on how they're told, stories of immigrant parents doing the best they can with the little they know about the "new country" can be funny indeed, as can stories describing old-fashioned parents' adherence to outdated ways. As a child of immigrant parents, this is something I can relate to personally. And on the face of it, it was *as if* this was the context of Nicholas's story.

But in the actual context here, a context in which I asked him to give me an example of why he thought he had—in his own words—a "good" mother, the story takes on a dark and ironic tone. The more he laughs, the more *sad* the story seems. And what really stands out is how out of touch he is with the impression he's making. In jumping up and down, mother's motive was to rid herself of him. Fundamental to attachment theory is our knowledge, as young children, that when we need our caregivers, we can go to them and they'll protect us.

Knowing that your mother wished you were never born—and that she can be cavalier in telling you so—is very painful. It goes with a sense of being abandoned by those who are supposed to love us most. For Nicholas, these feelings were cut off and suppressed, dealt with as if they didn't exist.

In keeping a painful story light, what comes across loud and clear is how Nicholas needs to *pretend*, how he deceives himself. I saw this not only in his words, but in his nonverbal behavior as well.

Let me unpack what happened in the brief moment between when he said,

"Well . . . my mother tried to abort me" and "Oh, the story is actually cute and funny. You see, she and I became very good friends later on." Just as he finished saying the words "my mother tried to abort me," it seemed he wanted to take it back. Shaking his head, with a look of disgust at the ridiculousness of what he'd just said, he began waving his hand dismissively, as if to wave away his own words, as if to explain how, really, it wasn't so bad, nothing like how it just sounded.

"Oh the story is actually cute and funny," he said, seemingly reassuring himself—or, perhaps, even reassuring me: How bad could it *possibly* have been? After all, "we became such good friends later on." It *couldn't* have been a big deal.

Self-deception happens a lot in trauma. We see this especially in psychotherapy with clients who minimize the impact of traumatic events, when they rationalize away painful experiences as having made them "all the stronger." Or, when they ignore the emotional content of their own traumatic history, when they use intellectualization as a defense, considering their experiences only cognitively. Feelings are cut out of the story, giving the impression that the client lives mostly "in his head."

We also see self-deception when survival in the home requires altering reality, to somehow make it more tolerable; the person forgets events that siblings recall with clarity. And, we see self-deception among those who recollect their own stories in detached clinical terms, relying on psychological jargon—so-called psychobabble—hiding from the vulnerability of their personal feelings.

British psychologist Peter Fonagy and colleagues (Allen et al., 2008) have studied attachment and psychotherapy extensively, looking at how those struggling in close relationships represent their own and others' intentions. Drawing on the work of philosopher Harry Frankfurt (2005), the authors noticed that in psychotherapy, and even in their everyday interactions, many clients function in *pretend mode*. Unlike lying, which has more to do with a deliberate misrepresentation of reality, the hallmark of pretend mode is a misrepresentation of intention—there is an *as if* quality to interactions with others.

In Nicholas's case, he told the story *as if* he intended to simply tell a light anecdote all along, as if the story were intended to give rise to lighthearted feelings, as if his mother's intentions arose simply from her immigrant background, and so on. At this early point in our work together, he had no insight into what—he would later discover—his own history meant to him, into the rejection he felt when his mother told him about the failed abortion attempts, or into how his resolve to keep his mother laughing came from concern she'd sink further into depression, or into how his father's temper meant fearing not only for his own life but also for his mother's. At this early point in treatment, the pain of his own history eluded him.

The term psychiatrist Judith Herman (1992) used is *doublethink*. Borrowed from George Orwell (1950), it's especially apt when considering the contradictory beliefs people have to hold when growing up in a traumatizing home. And it describes the self-deception that arises when people need to hold two opposing beliefs at the same time and accept the truth of them both. For example, "he loves me, he terrifies me" or "they harm me, they protect me."

When applied to attachment figures—people we're primed to trust—there can be no reconciling these competing sentiments without using mental gymnastics. Herman described how trauma survivors may alter perception and consciousness to accommodate a very confusing environment: "Through the practice of dissociation, voluntary thought suppression, minimization, and sometimes outright denial, they learn to alter an unbearable reality" (1992, p. 87).

How Trauma Stories Leak Out

Traumatic events are marked by so much pain, by such personal vulnerability that we go through great efforts to cover them up. But in the very routine of living, in the ups and downs of our daily interactions, our histories make their way into our lives and into our relationships.

Certainly this can happen in the context of major life events, like during developmental transitions (e.g., moving out, birth of a child) or during times of crisis (e.g., medical illness), but a variety of mundane events can act as triggers as well. Popular culture, in the form of literature, movies, and television series, all have the potential to provoke painful feelings and memories, and when they do, our stories have the potential to leak out.

Self-deception is by no means ironclad. Rather, the avoidance of traumatic experiences, feelings, and relationships is porous. We're able to stay guarded only so much and for only so long. And we *want* to stay guarded for only so long.

There's something very curious about Nicholas's abortion-attempt story.

Recall that *good* was one of the adjectives he used to describe his childhood relationship with his mother. And (consistent with AAI administration) after the listing of adjectives, I asked him to go back through them one at a time, to describe specific incidents or memories. What stories did he have of having experienced a good mother? How did he remember the relationship with her as good? Could he give me an example or two?

Surprisingly, it was precisely at *that* moment that he responded with, "Well . . . my mother tried to abort me." What an odd response. Why *then*?

Why would he tell me about the abortion attempt at *that* point in time? He had every opportunity to keep up the act. He could have easily told me a story about how his mother was a good cook, or that they'd had a vegetable garden in the backyard, both of which were true, and that somehow *those* made her a good mother. He could have told me about how, when he was young, his mother drove him to some of his activities, or that she sent him to Greek school on weekends, which he later described as good for his language development. He could have viewed her as good, simply on *that* basis.

But he relayed none of that. Instead, a story about a failed abortion attempt pops out, seemingly from thin air. What's going on here?

When Trauma Fragments Appear Unannounced

Nicholas's story helps illustrate the strange and often unpredictable way that trauma stories initially come to light. As I mentioned above, people go through enormous efforts to avoid facing traumatic experiences, feelings, and relationships. But there's a limit to how consistently one can stay guarded.

The concept of *trauma fragments* helps us understand how such stories surface. That is, they leak out in incomplete disembodied ways—in fragments. They appear out of context or disconnected from what's going on at the moment, as when painful memories show up seemingly out of nowhere. They may be incomplete or cut off from emotions, as we see with Nicholas, when—at this early point in treatment—his feelings of rejection, hurt, and abandonment are disconnected from his own painful story. They may come as a surprise or even a shock to the individual, bringing feelings of temporary distress. And they may come across as incoherent, relative to the person's usual way of talking.

In his three-volume series where he laid out the fundamentals of attachment theory, psychiatrist John Bowlby (1980) wrote:

> The exclusion of significant information, with the resulting deactivation of a behavioural system, may of course be less than complete. When that is so there are times when fragments of the information defensively excluded seep through so that fragments of the behaviour defensively deactivated become visible; or else feeling and other products of processing related to the behaviour reach consciousness, for example in the form of moods, memories, day dreams or night dreams. (pp. 65–66)

Given the strange out-of-context way in which trauma fragments appear in psychotherapy, let me emphasize that they can be *easy to miss*. Often, they show up briefly—words said under the person's breath. Or they come out in ways that give them a very different emotional tone, one that cuts off all feelings of vulnerability, rejection, hurt, or loss. Or, as in the case here, once the truth is out, it's taken back straight away.

Nicholas's immediate disavowal of a piece of his own past could make it easy for the therapist to collude with his defensive style, to conclude that Nicholas doesn't really view this as such a "big deal" after all.

So as a therapist, *noticing* trauma fragments is part and parcel of listening to the client, part of bearing witness in a way that's active and attentive.

People Feel Ambivalent About Their Trauma Stories

Still, I haven't answered the question, why *then*? What would compel Nicholas to tell me about the abortion attempt at that point in time? We can see that this disturbing revelation came unannounced, as if out of the blue, disconnected from his feelings. And we've talked about how the sudden unanticipated appearance of trauma fragments is actually quite common among trauma survivors. But what I haven't yet addressed is the issue of *ambivalence*.

As I pointed out earlier, we're able to stay guarded only so much, and for only so long. But equally important, we *want* to stay guarded for only so long.

In doing the AAI with Nicholas, in asking him to reflect on his childhood relationship with each caregiver, I was telling him I was interested in his relational world, in his personal experiences, and in the ways he made meaning of them. I was curious about him and how his early relationships have affected his choices as an adult. As someone who regularly casts himself in the role of entertaining others, he'd never really had much occasion to self-reflect. My sense was that, in part, there was something very important for him about an opportunity to unload a heavy burden.

And heavy it was. Later in our work together, I came to understand how rejection and abandonment were central themes in Nicholas's life. When he was about thirteen, his mother had had enough of the domestic violence and finally left the family. In the Greek community in which he grew up, this was unforgivable. And so, father forbade her from visiting or calling. Not that she tried all that hard. She'd moved out West, sending only yearly Christmas cards, and Nicholas didn't see her until he went to California for university, about five years later.

In effect, he was "aborted" from his mother's life. As a teenager, he was left to his own devices, to manage his father's drinking—which had worsened—and to take care of his younger brother, until his father remarried when Nicholas was in his last year of high school.

The AAI session, in which early in our work together I asked Nicholas to reflect on his childhood relationships with caregivers, was likely one of the first times in his life that anyone cared all that much about him. In the presence of an empathic ear, his guard down, it was as if he were saying, here's an example of my *not-so-good* mother, a mother who tried to abort me . . . more than once.

I've used this case illustration several times in my teaching. In London, England, a workshop attendee reflected on this case, saying that, after all, Nicholas was coming in for psychotherapy. Shouldn't we expect him, at least in part, to *want* to unload?

Ambivalence helps explain the contradictory motivations of trauma survivors. So often we see people in treatment who yearn to share their painful story but are afraid.

And they cycle between testing the waters, letting the therapist in just a bit—*can I trust you?*—only to put up their guard soon after, shutting discussion down, distancing themselves from close others and from vulnerable feelings.

It's Hard to Show Vulnerability, Even With the Therapist

Trauma makes us feel vulnerable. Triggers or reminders of one's painful history raise uncomfortable feelings: anxiety, fear, panic. And these feelings touch many areas of our lives, including home, family, and work. Painful emotions that come from traumatic experiences permeate relationships with our families, with our children, our parents and friends. That is to say, the feelings are interpersonal in nature.

When we talk about vulnerable feelings arising from trauma, what we're referring to is *relational vulnerability*. Feelings of rejection, loss, and betrayal all provoke a sense of vulnerability in relationships. This comes across especially when we're faced with the prospect of *depending on* close others.

In Chapter 1, I describe research pointing to the therapeutic relationship as central to good outcome. The vulnerability that trauma survivors feel in close relationships gets played out a lot in treatment. Psychotherapy is a context where feelings of dependency are stirred.

In therapy we feel understood, and we feel *mis*understood—we wish to share, but we feel exposed. We feel the therapist's empathy, but that may be unsettling, for it means someone cares. And if someone cares, someone can be lost.

When I did my clinical fellowship at Massachusetts General Hospital in the mid-1990s, some of our training concentrated on the psychiatric interview (Carlat, 2004). Typically carried out in the early stages of treatment, a good interview helps with diagnosis and treatment planning. And to do it well, clinicians focus on key areas in the client's life. One is the person's history of previous psychological treatments. Was the client in therapy before, and if so for how long? What modality? Outpatient or inpatient?

This is all useful to know. But what I've seen with trauma survivors is that, when reviewing previous therapies, it's most useful to find out what the treatment *relationships* were like. Because trauma affects so many areas of functioning (e.g., mood, eating, parenting, sexuality), a great many such clients have been in treatment before, for one reason or another. What was their prior experience of the therapy relationship? Did they feel like they were able to trust the clinician? What happened if they began to rely on the therapist—how did they experience that? Did it lead to a sense of disappointment, feeling judged or criticized, or feeling rejected? What happened when they disagreed with the clinician, and was there enough flexibility in the relationship to express it?

And, if the person had never before been in psychotherapy, then in *other* helping relationships, what feelings arose when they had to rely on someone? In other words, when in need, when in distress, what is their history of *depending on others*?

People with histories of interpersonal trauma really struggle with the idea of dependency, of relying on others. It provokes feelings of vulnerability. We can better appreciate that vulnerability by understanding how they experienced prior and current therapeutic relationships.

With Nicholas, vulnerability was a theme throughout our work. Especially early on, he would present his "funny side"—his version of armor—at the start of almost every meeting. But a few months in, this began to shift.

In one poignant session, we were discussing his brother. After their mom moved out West, when Nicholas was still a teenager, their dad's drinking worsened, and virtually every week either he or his younger brother would get beaten for some infraction. Father used a brown extension cord, stored in a supply cupboard near the kitchen, which, as part of the process, the child about to be beaten was expected to retrieve.

After one especially bad beating, one of them—either he or his brother—had multiple red marks on the skin, in the shape of the cord's electrical plug. The marks extended across the legs and thighs and required a few weeks to fully heal. And although Nicholas could clearly remember the marks, vividly describing their color, their shape and size, he couldn't recall whose body they were on, his or his brother's. *One* of them had to stay home from school for at least a week. Again, he just couldn't remember who.

It takes massive repression to confuse one's own body with someone else's. In that moment, Nicholas couldn't tell where his skin ended and his brother's began. He had literally disembodied his own emotional experience.

I asked him what he felt as he told me that story. What did he experience as he shared it with me? He didn't say much, initially. With his head in his hands, looking down, he appeared pensive. But after about a minute or two, and a heavy sigh, more than anything what I saw was a sadness he hadn't shown me before. He told me his brother had e-mailed him, out of the blue, a couple of weeks earlier; they hadn't spoken for a few years over a minor squabble. In time, he reached for a tissue and wiped his eyes, which were red. For the last few minutes of the session, he was rather muted, and soon we wrapped up.

Nicholas's reaction the following week was striking: He apologized for crying the week before. Apparently, he'd been so rattled by the session that afterward he sat in my waiting room for half an hour. And now he was sorry for, in his words, "losing it like a baby." So here he was, face to face with an important moment—a moment that had made him feel out of control and childish, a moment that was unanticipated, a moment that only the two of us had shared, and that made him feel vulnerable. And here I was, seeing his anxious reaction to having let his guard down.

In his family, maintaining composure was something he'd learned to do well. "Losing it"—composure, that is—meant feeling vulnerable in a way he could rarely allow himself, a way that was frightening. While this was by no means the first time he'd opened up, something did seem different here. I'd seen something about him, a vulnerability he showed no one. His sadness, his pain, the smallness he felt as a kid, and his ultimate inability to protect his brother—he hid these from everybody. And while he'd started to show me this side the week before, he had no idea what to make of it. He was exposed.

In response, I was mostly just curious. I invited him to *reflect on* last week's session. What was it like to cry? What was hard about it, what was uncomfortable about it, what made it different from his usual way of being? What did it mean to cry *in front of me*? What would make him imagine I expected "an apology" (as he put it)? And what did it feel like to talk about this with me, right here, right now?

To help Nicholas sit with this vulnerable moment, to help him look at it, feel it, make meaning of it, was to help him come to *bear* it. In his family of origin, crying was a punishable offense. To be seen as vulnerable . . . that was a big deal.

In a popular TED talk, and in her writings, mental health researcher Brené Brown emphasizes that, for interpersonal connection to happen, we must allow ourselves to be *seen*. The ability to be vulnerable in relationships is fundamental to finding and cultivating human connection. Brown, in fact, considers vulnerability to be "the cradle of the emotions and experiences that we crave. Vulnerability is the birthplace of love, belonging, joy, courage, empathy, and creativity" (2012, p. 34).

Mutual Avoidance: When Client *and* Therapist Avoid

Several years ago I attended a workshop in Toronto led by psychologist Anthony Mannarino, along with his colleague and coauthor psychiatrist Judith Cohen (Cohen & Mannarino, 2005; Cohen et al., 2006). Early in the training day, Mannarino told a story that left a strong impression on me as a therapist, so much so that I've made a point of sharing it with my supervisees since.

Describing his work with sexual abuse survivors, he told us about a school-age boy he used to work with, a child who'd previously been in psychotherapy for some time with mixed results. In one of their first sessions, Mannarino inquired gently about the nature of the prior treatment. He asked his young client to describe what he and the other clinician used to discuss in therapy. In particular, how did they talk about the sexual abuse? How did they address it, how did they work on it? The boy had been in psychotherapy for a few years because of the abuse, so the question was quite reasonable.

Confused, the child responded that, actually, he and his therapist had never discussed it—the topic hadn't come up in the earlier treatment. Mannarino gently queried further. How did the boy understand *why* they hadn't talked about it? To which the young client responded, he never thought his therapist *wanted* to talk about *that*.

We've been looking at *client* avoidance of traumatic experiences, feelings, and relationships, but equally important is the piece the therapist brings to the table. As uncomfortable as it is to discuss sexual abuse with adult survivors of trauma, it can be all the more challenging when working with young children. As I said in Chapter 1, clinicians and parents worry that talking about it will lead to retraumatizing the youngster. And fears like this can be enough to shut down important therapeutic work.

By *mutual avoidance*, I'm referring to a joint process, a co-construction of a space that feels unsafe—in this case, a space that says: this trauma is bigger than the both of us, and together, we'll agree *not* to look it, it's too frightening.

In therapy, this happens all too often, especially with clients reluctant to face their painful history. The therapist gets the message: don't go there, the client is just too scared. This can be enough to dissuade uncomfortable discussion for months or even years in treatment. And if therapists have their own insecurities about trauma-related topics, if they get triggered and show obvious discomfort, then the client gets the message: don't go there, this space is just not safe.

And sometimes, rightly or wrongly, we act on what we *imagine* the other is feeling. Based on our own vulnerabilities, we project intentions onto the other, ascribing to them what we feel as intolerable in ourselves. In the case of the sexually abused boy, it's entirely possible that he'd considered his former therapist as uninterested in his traumatic past, in part, because of his own discomfort with the topic.

Still, it's rarely only one-sided that clients avoid traumatic experiences, feelings, and relationships. When we see people in therapy for years, never actually getting to their deepest pains, both client *and* therapist bring something to the mix. One person's avoidance affects the other, and back again—it's cyclical.

Let's revisit the case of Nicholas. Recall that his sense of humor worked well for him, but it came at a price. It went along with a tendency to downplay vulnerable feelings, a reluctance to open up personally. He avoided his painful past, precluding intimacy in the present.

Recall also that, when we did the AAI, *good* was an adjective he used to describe his childhood relationship with his mother. And that after he listed his adjectives, I asked him to go back through them one at a time, to describe specific incidents or memories. What stories did he have of a good relationship with his mother? He replied with an anecdote about how his pregnant mother tried to abort him by jumping up and down, believing that doing so would terminate the pregnancy. As Nicholas recounted the story, he was laughing with gusto.

To help us think about the *mutual* aspect of avoidance, let's look at how I *responded* to him in that moment.

Oddly enough, I was smiling. I even chuckled at one brief point. Yet here's the curious thing: I don't find that story the least bit funny. And even at the time of its telling, I didn't find it funny. I felt uncomfortable, anxious. I also felt confused and—upon later reflection—sad for Nicholas.

But in the moment, I was behaving *as if* I found it funny. Like Nicholas, I was showing that same *as if* quality discussed earlier. My behavior belied what I was feeling inside.

I reflected on the session afterward, to consider what was going on for me at the time, to try to figure out my own motivations. And what I came to understand was that, in all likelihood, I was being *drawn in*. It was like I was being asked to collude with his way of describing his past, to minimize its emotional impact and importance—as if he was saying, in parentheses: *I'm laughing about it, now you laugh too.*

So I responded in kind, with a smile painted on my face. If you'd seen my thought balloon as he was speaking, it might have read, "I'm smiling, but I have no clue why."

And of course, the problem with this kind of collusive response is that it gives the message that this painful story—one that Nicholas came to understand very differently later on in our work—this story *was* really no big deal.

In *Attachment in Psychotherapy* (2007), psychologist David Wallin describes the *enactments* that occur in treatment. He wrote that the therapeutic relationship is influenced by both client and therapist. It's co-constructed. The unconscious needs and vulnerabilities of the two intersect, affecting treatment. Wallin wrote: "The patient's words may pull us in or push us away, open us up or shut us down, make us comfortable or heighten our anxiety. And, of course, our words to the patient have the same kind of impact" (p. 270).

Mutual avoidance is a kind of enactment, a tacit agreement to keep distant from experiences or feelings that make us feel vulnerable. It happens subtly, so it's easy to miss. It's important for therapists to *notice* when they're being drawn in, or to notice it soon afterward.

After the AAI session with Nicholas, I wondered about the interaction between him and me, reflecting on his telling of the abortion-attempt story and my response to it. I noticed the discrepancy between how the story made me feel and how I acted with him, and I was able to experience more genuinely the sadness and abandonment inherent in the story.

I also imagined that, over the years, Nicholas must have become quite skilled at getting the world to laugh along with him. Not a bad skill to have, mind you, but limiting—when it undermines the vulnerability needed for true intimacy.

CHAPTER 3

What Underlies Avoidance in Trauma?

The Tale of the Protective Mother

My father has always admired his aunt Kati, who saved his life. Raised Jewish, in Budapest, Hungary, he was a child during the Holocaust.

When my father was just eight years of age, his father was placed into forced labor, then into the concentration camp Buchenwald, never to be heard from again. About a year later, his mother was also taken to forced labor, rounded up with the other Jewish women in the neighborhood.

And with that, my school-age father and his younger sister found themselves frighteningly alone.

A day passed. Most of the Jewish adults in the neighborhood had now been taken away, and my father and his younger sister were left behind. But soon, my father's uncle arrived at the apartment where the two children remained, collected them, and brought them to the nearby flat he shared with his wife, Kati. Although the uncle was born Jewish, Kati was Catholic. And for some time, she'd been getting him to regularly attend church services with her, helping him evade suspicion about his Jewish background.

When Kati decided to risk her life for my father, she'd only known him for a very short time. At age twenty-three, new to the family, she would soon become instrumental in obtaining the false papers that helped my father survive. The situation felt perilous. At the time, in Second World War Hungary, any surname that wasn't ethnically Hungarian-sounding could arouse suspicion. My father's family worried the name Muller—very *un*-Hungarian-sounding— carried too much risk. They considered my father's identification documents a liability. The decision was made: he needed false papers.

Physically obtaining the documents was the easy part. Kati had a nephew in her family, a young boy like my father, whose surname was Pap, meaning priest. She quickly arranged for a copy of the boy's papers to be sent. But while the name was suitably non-Jewish sounding, unless the documents were signed and stamped by the Gestapo—permitting the designee to stay within the confines of Budapest—they'd be of little value. There was no way around it. Kati and my father would have to go to the train station to get the papers signed. They'd have to face the Gestapo directly.

Giving my young father no sense of what they were about to do, no warning of the dangers just ahead, thinking on her feet, with cool collectedness, Kati removed her wedding band and flirted unabashedly with the Gestapo official, promising him a rendezvous at the end of the day. Then, she matter-of-factly asked him to sign the papers.

And with that, they scurried out. Given how easy it would have been for the official to tell my father to drop his pants—common practice at the time— to determine if he was circumcised, and therefore Jewish, they were lucky to leave with their lives. If they had been caught, they would have been shot, then and there.

It's hard for my father not to get worked up when he tells the story. It's hard for me to hear—even though I've heard it my whole life.

In September of 2014, I went to Budapest, Hungary, for a visit. The purpose of my trip was to attend a countryside family wedding. There, a conversation with an old and ailing uncle would lead me to discover family I didn't know existed: a cousin of my father who'd never figured in any of his stories. Apparently, soon after the Second World War, Kati, then aged twenty-six, gave birth to a child, the first and only one she would have, a son they named Gyuri (George).

To me, this was big news. Indulging my rapid-fire questioning, my elderly uncle told me all he knew. He had met Gyuri years back, they'd had a couple of drinks, and as far as he understood, he was still alive. I diligently took down the phone numbers of a few relatives who might have information on his where-abouts, and that night, despite my fatigue, I slept restlessly.

I thought of how Gyuri had grown up with Kati. He knew her—my great aunt, who'd unflinchingly saved my father's life. I'd heard so much about her, I had a clear vision of who she was: strong, gutsy, quick thinking. I was determined—I would get to know her through his eyes.

I rescheduled my flight and commitments for the remainder of the week. And in my stilted Hungarian, after several false starts, I managed to track down Gyuri over the next couple of days, arranging a meeting point on the Danube, in downtown Budapest.

Over lunch and a drive into the country, Gyuri and I talked at length about growing up in postwar communist Hungary, about family from long ago. And soon, either at his suggestion or mine, we found ourselves walking through the cemetery where his parents were buried, the Catholic cemetery.

We walked to Kati's grave, soon replacing the dried flowers on the tomb-stone with fresh ones we'd purchased on the way in. He shared the few stories he remembered of his mother, painting a portrait of someone who was, more than anything, distant, reserved, silent—a woman consumed by the burdens of making ends meet. In his home, there were few family traditions, few stories, virtually no recognition of the past. His parents were old seeming, he said—detached from one another and from him; his family was disengaged. And more to the point, there was never discussion of the war, or the Holocaust, or the family's Jewish background. It was all held in secrecy.

And then he asked me what I knew. What was my understanding of the family, from the stories I'd been told? What could I tell him about his mother? With some trepidation (I didn't know how he'd respond), in all the detail I could remember, I shared the story of his mother's willingness to put her life on the line for my father. How she, of her own accord, *protected* my father, how she did so at enormous personal risk.

Later that evening, back at his apartment, as we shared a meal of *rakott krumpli*, a traditional potato dish, and beer, he asked me to tell him the story again, which I did. He had a lot of questions. But as he was a retired police officer, with a good poker face, it was hard to know *how* he understood the two Katis: one collected, courageous, selfless; the other, the mother he knew, the one who raised him, secretive, closed off, distant. It was confusing for him. He struggled to understand my father's version of his mother. How could that have been the same person he grew up with? It was confusing for me too.

How can someone so actively protective also be so passive and distancing? How can one willing to take a dangerous risk for family in one context become so aloof and avoidant in another? And how can someone ready to confront life-threatening truths retreat from the painful ones?

Two versions of my great aunt . . . not what I'd expected to find.

Avoidance as an Act of Protectiveness

Our closest relationships keep us alive. This was an insight of John Bowlby's (1980, 1988), and he spent the better part of his career as a psychiatrist writing about and teaching the ins and outs of attachment theory, an approach to understanding human behavior that has shaped individual and family psychotherapy, developmental psychiatry, and social psychology.

In Bowlby's view, *attachment* is a behavioral system of seeking protection and maintaining closeness to primary caregivers at times of perceived threat or danger. As young children, we turn to our parents when we're in distress. From an evolutionary standpoint, we're primed to do so because our very survival depends on it. To reach adulthood, our parents represent our best odds.

At its core, attachment theory is about protection: the motivation for children to seek the protection of their caregivers, and the motivation for caregivers to provide that protection—these are fundamental to survival.

And most of the time, staying near our caregivers is indeed what works best. But regardless of the quality of the parenting, children will do whatever is necessary to maintain that relationship. It's the relationship that keeps them alive, regardless of how painful, confusing, or inadequate.

This is why we see children who defend their parents no matter how troubled the adults are. It's why we see scenarios where, as therapists, we call Child Protective Services in response to alleged child abuse, only to find a few days later, when follow-up occurs between child and child-protection worker, allegations have been dropped. And the victim has even started doubting the truth of their own account.

Some of our stories are too frightening to deal with directly, too distressing, terrifying. In some families, recounting painful memories or experiences is emotionally unbearable; expressing vulnerable feelings seems dangerous. Families like these cope by relying on avoidance.

When we fear our own personal experiences, avoidance can be a means of protecting ourselves. And when expressing vulnerable feelings is intolerable to the relationship, when it seems that doing so will disturb or alienate those closest to us, avoidance can be a way of protecting others.

We protect our primary relationships. When the truth is dangerous to those relationships, we edit—or avoid—the truth, rather than risk the relationship.

Guarding the Family Secret

Sweeping family secrets under the rug is a theme I hear a lot from my clients. It's how many families survive, a concealment protecting everyone from memories they'd rather forget, from feelings they'd just as soon banish.

And it's an idea that's helped me better understand some of my extended family in Hungary. Traumatized by the Holocaust, they, like so many others, promised never to speak of the war, the concentration camps, the personal suffering. Avoidance of the past was a way of protecting their families, a means of survival.

Secretive families often come across as anemic, emotionally impoverished. There's a sense of disengagement that keeps things stable and holds painful feelings at bay. Although it protects the family, it also means much cannot be discussed, so there are holes in the narrative. There's a sense the family environment lacks vitality or color. There's a resistance to family storytelling.

Developmental psychologist Robyn Fivush and colleagues (Bohanek et al., 2009; Fivush & Sales, 2006) conducted a series of elegant studies on how families reminisce and construct stories. For example, how do families converse during dinnertime? How do they discuss the past? How do they address stressful or difficult events?

Among their findings, creating coherent narratives about life experiences was related to better psychological and physical health. Bohanek et al. wrote: "Mothers who reminisce about the past in more elaborate ways, providing rich detail and confirming and eliciting their children's participation, have children who show higher levels of emotional understanding and regulation. Studies have confirmed that maternal elaboration is the critical dimension in predicting child outcome" (2009, p. 491).

In families where coherent personal narratives are shared with children, storytelling models vulnerability. It conveys that to be human, is to have a range of feelings about one's own history, that we all have many parts to ourselves, some painful to acknowledge, some less than admirable.

My students and I have recently blogged about the importance of family storytelling (Carter-Simmons, 2013), explaining that stories pass on life lessons, instilling a sense of inner capability. And the shared history and time taken to tell stories also fill the need to connect, providing, in Fivush's view, a sense of belonging in our families—that we're part of something larger than ourselves.

In secretive families, stories don't get told—they're hidden away. And when they somehow appear, they're whitewashed. Personal sharing is considered too dangerous to family relationships.

And then there are the landmines: Topics that come up but have to be navigated around, to stave off family blowups, conflicts, or unpredictable reactions. Several years back, a client of mine had a cousin who committed suicide. After years of wrestling with depression, he finally reached a point of despair. The cousin was found dead in the basement of the family home—he'd hanged himself.

My client discussed the loss in great detail in therapy, but in the process of doing so, he said he was amazed at how, after the funeral, no one talked about his cousin—not his parents, not his siblings, not the grandparents. It quickly became a taboo topic, and the discomfort was especially palpable at Christmas. The cousin's birthday happened to be Christmas Day.

In this way, the cousin was relegated to the world of the nonexistent—no remembrance, no mentioning of his birthday, no discussion of his death, no space to discuss anything but vacuous platitudes at Christmas dinner, platitudes my client initially found infuriating and, as we worked it through, later found sad.

When Loyalty Prevails

In many families, as in social systems more broadly, the expectation is one of allegiance, a sense of duty to the group. This kind of loyalty protects one another, protects relationships in the family—it protects the family's ideals and values, and the image it projects to others.

Difficulties arise when family loyalty runs counter to the truth. Painful realities threaten the idealized story. When they do, when they contradict the image of celebrated family members, many respond by turning a blind eye.

I recently worked with a young man from a well-to-do family, from the American Southwest. He struggled with depression for many years, finding himself in a never-ending part-time university degree program, but telling his family that he'd graduated a couple of years earlier. As a child, when he was viewed as misbehaving, his mother, a physician, would lock him in the closet without food or access to a toilet for hours on end. His father, a well-loved pastor in their church, was often absent, working in the Albuquerque community where they lived.

For my client, painful as it was to make sense of the abusive parenting, what he struggled with particularly was the reaction of his father when he was confronted with the truth. As a teenager, just prior to his first depression, he questioned: *How could you not have known what was going on in your own home?* His father's reaction? *She's your mother. Pray for her!* And with chagrin, alongside his father, my client did just that, not knowing anything else.

No charges were laid. And for years my client was convinced *he* was the crazy one for not being grateful enough. He had come from a prominent family, after all—what did *he* have to complain about? And he held inside a punishing sense of shame for having betrayed his mother, for bad-mouthing the family name, sometimes even questioning whether he'd dreamt it all up.

Telling the truth of one's own traumatic experiences can feel like an act of disloyalty. This is precisely why *validation* is so important when working with trauma survivors, why therapists need to listen strenuously and nonjudgmentally when clients do share, why the role of the therapist, in part, is to bear witness to loss and suffering. Telling the truth can make us feel like we're hurting those we're supposed to love.

Like with families, in many institutions, the expectation is loyalty to the group, a loyalty that protects members. In police and military systems, the so-called blue wall of silence is an unwritten code to protect fellow police officers from investigation and uncomfortable scrutiny. Writer Bill Berkowitz (2015) described the code as the practice of closing ranks around one another, clamming up in the face of injustice, protecting one's own. It's a sense of loyalty that contributes to high levels of domestic violence in the homes of many police officers (Hope & Roslin, 2015; Roslin, 2017) and that contributes to stigma when police officers suffer from work-induced posttraumatic stress disorder (PTSD).

A telling report by Ontario, Canada, ombudsman André Marin (2012), *In the Line of Duty*, concludes that officers faced with the realities of mental illness are encouraged to "suck it up." As one staff development and training officer put it:

> You are supposed to be this tough, unfeeling, cool, collected officer all the time. You're in the public. You're dealing with something that's really horrific. It's not supposed to bother you. But it does. And it bothers some people more than others. The reason I don't show my emotions when I'm out on the street in front of the public is because I'm not supposed to do that as a police officer. So right there, it is stigma management in my head. So is there a stigma attached to mental illness? Absolutely there is, and it's not just policing. There is a stigma associated to mental illness in any employment. But you don't want to be seen as being weak. (p. 80)

In contexts demanding high levels of loyalty, there's a strong draw toward silence on interpersonal trauma and its consequences. As I said above, telling the truth about one's own traumatic experiences can feel like an act of disloyalty. The expectation is one of allegiance, a sense of duty to the group. Loyalty protects the group, its ideals and image. But the price can be high.

What does it mean to be a good soldier? In the treatment of veterans, social worker Susan Knoedel (2009) has documented the important role of military culture on military sexual trauma (MST), a term coined by the U.S. Department of Defense to capture the different forms of sexual maltreatment reported by military personnel (Burgess, Slattery, & Herlihy, 2013). In basic training, implicit messages emphasize loyalty to the group: subsuming one's own needs to the mission at hand, acceptance of authority, being "owned" by the military, and refusal to divulge negative information about peers (Knoedel, 2009).

When we consider the expectation of loyalty, alongside that of trauma-related silence in military culture, we see why former U.S. defense-secretary Chuck Hagel declared MST a clear threat to the lives and well-being of service members, with one in four females and one in ten males in the military reporting one or more incidents (Herlihy & Burgess, 2014).

Writing an impassioned appeal in the *New York Times* about how his daughter, a marine, had been beaten, raped, and sodomized by a superior officer, former U.S. marine Gary Noling (2016) described the poor treatment victims receive if they don't stay silent. He wrote that, from 2009 to 2015, 25 percent of service members leaving the military, after reporting sexual assault, had been discharged because of some kind of "misconduct," and that about a third of those discharges were related to alcohol or drug use, often linked to PTSD.

In their work on MST, researchers Patricia Herlihy and Ann Burgess (Burgess et al., 2013; Herlihy & Burgess, 2014) documented a poignant case:

> Michael, a Vietnam war veteran, was raped in 1974 at the Whiteman Air Force Base in Missouri, a year after his graduation from high school. He describes how three servicemen waited in the dark and struck him from behind as he walked past a construction site on the base. He was knocked unconscious, beaten and sodomized. . . . Michael, like many victims of MST, suffered in silence throughout his 20-year career as a communications specialist. (Herlihy & Burgess, 2014, p. 11)

Afraid of the consequences of disloyalty, service members so often choose not to report MST. Underscoring the price he paid for *his* silence, Michael stated: "I lived with this beast in my head for nearly 30 years before telling my wife and going for counselling" (Burgess et al., 2013, p. 23).

When We Protect Ourselves From Our Own Trauma Histories

Earlier in this chapter, I said that some of our stories are too frightening to deal with directly. Expressing vulnerable feelings can feel dangerous to our important relationships. Avoidance can be a way of protecting relationships, and important others, from the truth.

But when we find it unbearable to feel, to remember, or even to think about our own personal experiences, avoidance can be a way of protecting *ourselves* as well.

Let's consider the case of Annette. In her mid-thirties, she was referred to me with a dual diagnosis of addiction (heavy marijuana use) along with psychological trauma from a rape during her third year of university in Ohio. As a child, her parents argued relentlessly, and although her mother was a mediator in high-conflict labor disputes—flying here and there for work—it was Annette who would cool things down at home. In her teenage years, she would often physically separate her parents, especially when the shouting became frightening for her younger sister.

An outstanding athlete in high school, she would go running when she needed to calm herself, and she joined the volleyball team in university. At age twenty, she was drugged and raped by her on/off boyfriend. She stopped going to practices, finding it difficult to motivate herself, steadily gaining weight over the next couple of years, and she eventually dropped all her classes.

In the section below, taken from about a month into our work together, Annette tells me about the day her mother finally left the family. Annette was sixteen then. Throughout her parents' tumultuous relationship, her mom would leave for weeks at a time, with no one in the family knowing where she was exactly or when she would return. But this time, it affected Annette in a way it never had before:

I remember when she left. She took her luggage and her fancy pink cosmetics case and told us, "I'm just leaving for a few weeks. My clients need me." And I said, "Sure I'll see you later." And it was just me and my little sister at home, and my sister shouted, "No don't. Mommy come back," and I'm like, "Hey, just take it easy, she's only going for a few weeks, she'll be back, don't worry about it." And later on, when my dad came home, he got angry. He was shouting at us for letting her leave. He told us we shouldn't have let her. And I was like, "No, don't be crazy, she just left for a few weeks and she'll be back; she goes all the time, so it's nothing to make a big issue of." I mean, it was true, she would leave for a few weeks all the time and come back. It was fine. We really were quite fine with that. But my dad was really upset, and me and him couldn't get along at first 'cause he was like, "What's wrong with you? You don't realize what's going on?" And I was like, "You don't know what's going on either. Don't worry for no good reason!"

But then a year went by. And then it was another year, and then another. And, it was just so much time. And she didn't answer any of my letters. It was just so much time . . . so much waiting (long pause) . . . I don't think she's *ever* coming back.

After Annette shared this story with me, particularly toward the end, she was uncharacteristically quiet, somber. I asked her what was going on for her right then. What was it like to tell me about the time her mother left and moved away?

As we talked about it, it seemed she couldn't really say *what* exactly she was feeling inside. But this session paved the way for some important work we would embark on soon enough. The theme of loss became important in the therapy—so many losses: her trust in women, her trust in men, her sense of her own sexuality, her university years, her mother who never did return.

But this early point was just one month into treatment. And it's interesting to look a little more closely at the transcript. What does it tell us about this young woman? How does she protect herself from her own story? How does she try to cool down her own feelings, to make them more tolerable?

Relax . . . don't worry about it . . . don't be silly . . . nothing to make a big issue of . . . it was fine . . . we were really quite fine . . . don't worry for no good reason— all language showing a desperate attempt to reassure herself, as in: everything is okay, I'll be okay. But, of course, she didn't *feel* okay. She was starting to have medical problems, mostly related to her obesity. And she'd had to drop out of university and leave Ohio, getting as far as possible from where she'd been abandoned as a teenager, and from where she'd been assaulted as a young woman.

And like I described in Chapter 2, there's an *as if* quality here. When in distress, in the face of loss, Annette *pretended* to herself, acting as if everything was just fine. This was precisely how she managed her feelings toward the rape as well. Later in the treatment, when she decided she wanted to try dating again, I suggested she wait a while, and we began the painful work of unpacking her feelings toward sex, the sexual assault, and her ex-boyfriend, all of which raised feelings that frightened her.

Notice also the language that Annette recalls her family using. Their fears are borne out in the end. Little sister: *No don't. Mommy come back.* And father: *What's wrong with you, you don't realize what's going on?* Both speak to the painful truth, a permanent loss that, to Annette, had been hiding in plain sight.

Later as we worked through a great many losses, and as she connected to her sadness, these truths no longer eluded her. We see her starting to do this work, at the end of the session, when she says that after her mother left, a year went by, and then another year. Her mother never did respond to the letters mailed to her. Annette pauses, as she repeats that so much time had passed, so much waiting.

And then it dawns on her: *I don't think she's <u>ever</u> coming back.*

When Culture Suppresses Awareness of Trauma

Remembering Our Own History

How do we think about our own history, how do we refer to it, remember it? If we've suffered greatly, do we label it as traumatic? Or, do we try to erase it altogether, perhaps viewing it as mundane? *It's what we all went through . . . forget about it.* In short, how do we narrate our own past?

Here, the importance of cultural and historical context has to be emphasized. Cultural forces suppress awareness of trauma. Culture and history define and shape trauma narratives. They support them, they maintain them. They shut them down.

Our understanding of our history is always in context. Cultural forces affect the character of our stories, and we're often unaware of those forces. Depending on the time and place we live in, similar life experiences may or may not be viewed as traumatic. Our cultural backdrop plays an important role in whether we ignore or minimize traumatic life experiences. Do we stop ourselves from owning our history, from engaging in acts of remembrance, from incorporating our past into our personal identities?

As I pointed out earlier in this chapter, after the Second World War many European Jews were traumatized by the Holocaust. The ones from my own extended family who remained in Hungary mostly lived a minimally Jewish existence. Some joined the communist party as a means of forging a new identity, and some shed themselves completely of the past. My great uncle legally changed the "Jewish-sounding" surname, Muller, to the less conspicuous Dioszegi, meaning literally, "from Dioszeg," the town where he was born.

And, as I discovered on my visit to Hungary a few years ago, he and my great aunt Kati chose *never* to discuss the war, the Holocaust, or the family's Jewish background—nothing from their frightening past. There were few shared family traditions, few stories—a climate of secrecy, in part, I imagine, to protect their young family from the past, but in part because of the postwar cultural milieu.

To blend in, a great many European Jews changed their names and baptized their children, deciding they would remove all remnants of the past. They would promise to "keep the secret," in the words of Toronto writer John Lorinc (2008). In this way, cultural forces have enormous power to whitewash the truth of the past.

When the Powerful Manipulate Trauma Awareness

As I've been discussing, our willingness to view our most harrowing life experiences as traumatic depends, in part, on the time and place we live. This is important because how we characterize these experiences affects how we see ourselves. Remembering and acknowledging the truth can mean connection with similar others, as we see in domestic violence survivor groups. It can also mean culturally sanctioned remembrance for service men and women who have fallen. And it can mean shared national, religious, and ethnic identity surrounding themes of loss and mourning.

Community plays an immense role in recovery from trauma, and community support can't come about unless the dominant culture acknowledges the truth of the suffering some have endured. In *Trauma and Recovery* (1992), psychiatrist Judith Herman wrote:

> Returning soldiers have always been exquisitely sensitive to the degree of support they encounter at home. Returning soldiers look for tangible evidence of public recognition. After every war soldiers have expressed resentment at the general lack of public awareness, interest, and attention; they fear their sacrifices will be quickly forgotten. After the First World War, veterans bitterly referred to their war as the "Great Unmentionable." When veterans' groups organize, their first efforts are to ensure that their ordeals will not disappear from pubic memory. (p. 70)

But public memory is elusive and fleeting and can be swayed. When politically expedient, those in dominant positions of power shape the nature of discourse. Truth can be manipulated, and victims can be cast as perpetrators.

This rhetorical sleight-of-hand is often used on trauma survivors. The blaming of victims for sexual assault, or *victim blame*, has been well documented (Muller, Caldwell, & Hunter, 1993, 1994, 1995). For many, casting victims as perpetrators is convenient. It changes the conversation, it denies responsibility. And throughout history, there are numerous examples of women in particular, seeking justice for sexual assault, slammed in the court of public opinion (Goldberg, 2016).

Governments, interest groups, and power brokers fiddle with collective memory, manipulating what we think of as trauma. And this can be carried out on a vast scale. As cultural critic and literature professor Edward Said pointed out, memory can be controlled by those in power, and widespread awareness or ignorance of traumatic events can be regulated. In Said's view, memory can be used selectively to manipulate facts on the national past, elevating some aspects and suppressing others. Memory is something to be "used, misused, and exploited, rather than something that sits inertly there for each person to possess and contain" (2005, p. 259).

What we label as "trauma" depends very much on the storyteller, how they frame the telling of the story.

Of course, this can be exploited for nefarious purposes, especially in a strongman regime. A haunting 2009 documentary by anthropologist Robert Lemelson tells how more than half a million people were secretly killed when Indonesia's General Suharto purged the country of suspected "communists." Remarkably, government propaganda successfully suppressed historic events, casting the victims as perpetrators, leading to widespread ignorance of the truth (Lemelson, 2009).

There are countless similar examples in history, and across the globe, but one I find important as a Canadian is my own country's complacence in cultural genocide denial. As writer Scott Gilmore (2015) has pointed out, Canada enjoys an image of progressive tolerance throughout the world. Its dirty little secret? Treatment of its aboriginal population makes for a race problem that rivals that of the United States.

Incarceration rates of Aboriginal Canadians are ten times that of the national rate; the homicide rate is over six times the national rate. And Canada's residential school system—lasting over a hundred years until 1996—which had the express purpose of removing native children from their culture, meant that almost a third of all aboriginal youth were taken from their family homes, deprived of their languages, and subjected to remarkably high levels of physical and sexual abuse by staff.

In 2008, Prime Minister Stephen Harper issued an apology on behalf of the Canadian government for the residential school system, and in 2015, the Truth and Reconciliation Commission found that Canada committed cultural genocide against its indigenous population.

Still, a number of respected Canadian columnists balked at the term *cultural genocide*, despite—or because of—deliberate use of the term by Canada's Supreme Court chief justice. One columnist even questioned whether

Canada was any guiltier than any other country that had tried to eradicate its indigenous culture (as if *that* made it morally justifiable) (Simpson, 2015). He referred to a focus on this part of our collective history as "wallowing," maintaining that we shouldn't "fixate" so much on the past.

In a fiery rebuttal in *Now* magazine, social activist and writer Bernie Farber explained: "No amount of research, no accounting of first-hand memories by thousands of aboriginal residential school survivors seems enough to change deniers' refusal to accept our historical role in attempting to wipe out indigenous people and their culture from our land" (2015, p. 17).

Farber concluded: "It's time to accept the undeniable truth if we're serious about reconciliation" (p. 17).

My point exactly. We move forward only when we face the truth of the past.

CHAPTER 4

The Dangers of Rushing In: When the Client-Therapist Relationship Is Unprepared

A Traumatizing Therapy

When people are traumatized by overwhelming life events, they're left raw and unstable, uncertain about how to move forward. They want to get better but have no idea how. Some feel alone with little guidance. They come across many viewpoints: self-help gurus, internet advice, and quick fixes. From friends, family, and professionals, they receive contradictory advice. They're left scratching their heads in confusion.

David Morris felt traumatized by his therapy. A former marine infantry officer, he'd narrowly escaped death several times, including once by an IED—an improvised explosive device—in southern Baghdad, in 2007. Morris realized he needed help years later, after he found himself pacing the lobby of a movie theater, scrutinizing peoples' hands, fearing they were carrying weapons. He'd been watching a movie with his girlfriend, there had been an on-screen explosion, and he bolted out.

About a year later, symptoms weren't lifting, and Morris went to the San

Diego VA hospital for treatment. In an account of his experiences there, it's clear it didn't take long for therapy to go off the rails: "My first session began with my therapist, a graduate student finishing up his doctorate in clinical psychology, offering a kind of apology. 'Now I'm probably going to make some mistakes and say some stupid things,' he said. 'Are you going to be O.K. with that?'" (Morris, 2015a).

Describing those who'd worked with him at the VA as young, naïve, inexperienced, and "illiterate" about the war on terror, Morris's account suggests that he neither trusted his therapist nor felt comfortable launching into the painful work they'd soon embark on, which focused on telling and retelling his traumatic experiences with virtually no preparation.

He referred to the clinician as being "like a young salesman," who was, in essence, selling him on the very idea of therapy. Once treatment began, far from feeling like he had a partner to share in the pain of his trauma—one who could help him make sense of the issues—Morris felt alone in the process.

And he went from considering therapy unhelpful to viewing it as downright retribution: "I began to think of the treatment not as therapy so much as punishment. Penance" (Morris, 2015b, p. 181).

After a few weeks, his symptoms progressively worsened, to the point of him destroying his own cell phone in abject rage. And Morris quit treatment, his therapist trying to sell him on the method right to the end. Soon enough, he began therapy anew. This time it was a group model, with two therapists whom he experienced as understanding, patient, authoritative, and collaborative, interested in helping him examine tough issues important to him.

Following a treatment he found useful, Morris ultimately concluded: "Most people cannot emerge from post-traumatic stress by simply gutting it out. Chronic PTSD is a life-threatening event and has to be treated or intensively managed by loved ones. During treatment, you must continue to fight, continue to seek insights into your experience, continue to read and to introspect, continue to seek out the company and advice of others. The community of survivors is a real thing" (2015b, p. 211).

Trauma therapy can't happen without safety. And without basic trust in the therapeutic relationship, it's doomed. Who can feel safe discussing their most personal, traumatic experiences without feeling confident the therapist can handle it?

Before launching into trauma therapy, before focusing on overwhelming experiences or painful losses, before reflecting on deeper hurts, fears, and vulnerabilities, in short, before opening up at all, trauma survivors must feel a sense of *containment*. For therapists, this is an important element when *pacing the process of opening up*. Facilitating a sense of containment in the therapeutic relationship makes it possible for the client to share and feel vulnerable. I'll say more about how to provide containment, but first let me share a story about a Canadian Air Force pilot.

Providing Containment in the Therapeutic Relationship

A few years ago, I worked with a Canadian pilot in therapy. He'd been referred to me because his wife's psychiatrist was worried. In her therapy sessions, the wife had been complaining about her husband's prescription drug abuse and unpredictable rages. In addition, there was a lack of sexual intimacy in their marriage for the past several months. Also concerning—because it was out of character for him—the pilot was now regularly invoking God into their discussions. One day, he e-mailed his wife four words: *I want to separate.*

His wife, thoroughly practical, recognized how odd this all was, And was more concerned for his mental health than anything. She told me that her husband had lost six of his closest friends in a recent helicopter accident in Afghanistan. Now stationed in Toronto, although he was supposed to be participating in a local training program, he was calling in sick and staying home in bed, seemingly depressed, highly agitated. And he'd even lost interest in seeing his teenage daughter from his previous marriage. This was all unlike him.

I worked with the pilot for about eight months before he was stationed elsewhere. But in our very first session, as we discussed an unrelated topic, he blurted out that he was sexually abused at age nine. He'd been forced to perform fellatio on his male babysitter. This, he followed with a question: *Is that why I'm so fucked up?*

I told him that, frankly, I didn't know, I didn't know him just yet, so I really couldn't say, but that I'd try to help him figure it out. And about two months into our work together, we did start to unpack what had happened with the babysitter: what he felt about it, and what he worried it said about him. But at that earlier point in our work together, I was just trying to forge a connection. This fellow was someone who, I came to realize, had never talked about his sexual abuse with anyone. Other than his high school girlfriend, he'd never shared his secret with friends or family, or with his concerned wife.

Psychological containment is about feeling safe and secure in the therapeutic space. It's about feeling confident in the therapist as a capable guide, one who's been around the block. The clinician empathizes with the client's pain but at the same time isn't undone by it. The space can *hold* disturbing feelings, not judge, minimize, or become overwhelmed by them. Only when there's basic trust in the therapeutic relationship can clients openly share their most deeply held experiences.

This is what is meant by a *holding environment*: the sense that the therapeutic space is strong enough to contain the pains that clients, on their own, find unbearable. Before any therapy can happen, the client has to feel safety and confidence in the relationship (Muller, 2010). They must feel a sense of containment.

When treatment doesn't work out, it's so often because the relationship is off. Psychiatrist Michael Franz Basch, who taught at the Chicago Institute for Psychoanalysis, wrote that therapist unwillingness or inability to navigate challenges in the relationship is the most common reason for unsuccessful therapy, for treatment becoming a "circular, repetitive recounting of symptoms" (1980, p. 40).

As I said in Chapter 1, since the late 1970s we've had rigorous meta-analyses—large-scale reviews that gather findings across studies—on the benefits of psychotherapy (Smith & Glass, 1977; Smith et al., 1980). Bringing together these reviews with a great many other meta-analyses, psychologist Bruce Wampold in *The Great Psychotherapy Debate* (2001) found that relationship factors such as the alliance between clinician and client were much more important in a successful treatment than anything else the therapist could control. And these findings have been corroborated repeatedly. A strong therapist-client relationship with acceptance, empathy, warmth, and encouragement was shown to be more helpful than the specific school of thought therapists used. In short, the relationship lies at the heart of psychotherapy.

And when trust in others has been badly damaged, as is so often the case with interpersonal trauma, the therapeutic relationship becomes all the more important. This is something emphasized by Noi Quao, who manages traumatic event support services at Morneau Shepell, a large North American provider of employee assistance and human resources services. In an interview I conducted with him, Quao expressed clear views on which characteristics typified the most skilled of their trauma counselors: "They have an excellent ability to connect, and to make adjustments if it seems that a disconnection has happened. Also, they listen, and that helps them connect too. They don't come in from on-high, nor are they self-effacing either. They invite people in, they are interactive. Problems happen when they can't establish rapport from the start, and when they can't find a way to connect" (personal communication, September 28, 2016).

A good treatment relationship can take a long time to develop. Many clients struggle in therapy, not knowing *how* to trust the therapist, so it can be slow.

In his text on treating people with complex PTSD, *Rebuilding Shattered Lives* (2011), psychiatrist James Chu wrote that the fragile nature of this trust can last months, sometimes years, where "even attempts to empathize and expressions of caring can be misunderstood as threatening or intrusive by patients who have grown up in environments of pervasive victimization" (p. 163).

When we invite our clients to trust us, we expect a lot. To help clinicians appreciate just how tall an order this is, Chu suggests a mental exercise. Imagine being asked to climb up to the rooftop with your therapist. There, you must concentrate on feeling light as air. Then join hands with the other person, and . . . together step off. Have faith that somehow, you'll float to the ground. If you had any sense at all, Chu wrote, "you'd decline the invitation and come back down by conventional means" (2011, p. 162).

Before clients can feel comfortable opening up, they must feel contained in the therapeutic relationship. This helps pace the process of trauma therapy. Why, then, do we see therapists and clients alike making the mistake of rushing in? Early in treatment, without testing the waters, with little more than a fledgling relationship . . . With no real sense of safety, no feeling of containment just yet, one or both members of the partnership hurry in?

And soon enough, both feel in over their heads. We can see this sometimes stemming from the client, and sometimes from the therapist.

When the Client Rushes In:
How to Provide Containment

Early in treatment, some people arrive ready to *rush into* the details of their traumatic history. Having held in their disturbing stories for so long, having held their feelings at bay, they hope that finally someone is willing to listen, as if all that remained were to unload the burden and somehow everything would be alright.

But without basic trust in the therapeutic relationship, it can be counter-productive for clients to hasten disclosure of their traumatic experiences. A case comes to mind of a junior lawyer who was referred to me by one of her senior partners in a respected downtown firm. Described as quick to anger, only days earlier she had physically assaulted a colleague at work. No charges were pressed, but she was required to seek treatment. Later, I came to under-stand the assault arose from a lovers' quarrel.

The original inquiry into treatment came from the human resources person-nel at the firm. When I heard language from them like "counseling required" and "anger management," I confess I made assumptions. I expected a certain defensiveness or disengagement in the client, dry one-word answers perhaps—I wasn't sure, but something to that effect. Client reactions like these are com-mon among those who feel forced into treatment.

On the contrary, what I found felt rather like a monsoon. In a cascade of words, what came across more than anything was just how desperately she wanted to be heard. And right there, not fifteen minutes into our first session, I would learn about a history of sexual abuse from her father, from her mother, beatings from both, a cruel and sadistic relationship between her parents toward one another, and a retreat into books, an imaginative world of fiction where she could find a semblance of peace. So it went, throughout the remainder of the session, her talking over my feeble attempts to interject. She rushed to tell me everything. And I listened closely, yes—still, it seemed, I wasn't quite giving her what she needed.

And then, I didn't hear from her for the next six months.

When she finally did reemerge, it was because there had been another vio-lent outburst at work, and she was in danger of losing her job. When we now met, I asked her about her decision six months earlier not to return: How did she arrive at that? What had she experienced in the aftermath of our meeting?

In fact, she'd already made up her mind to drop the whole thing in the eleva-tor ride down, immediately after our first session. And she ignored the messages I left her regarding follow-up; she hoped her anger problems would go away on their own.

But we'd now embark upon trauma therapy, lasting for the next two years.

And the issue of her dropping out, or threatening to drop out of treatment—especially when her feelings overwhelmed her—became an important theme. Simply put, relationships terrified her. In fact, it was particularly when she felt understood by me, when she found me empathic, when she felt she could depend on me, that she'd threaten to drop out.

It's fortunate she chose to call back, and perhaps she did so because, after all, she'd felt listened to. But there are a great many clients who wouldn't call back, representing a lost opportunity for growth. This case shows how important it is to be prepared for clients who hurry in, without giving themselves or anyone else fair warning. Let's look at this idea in detail.

Recall the case of the Canadian air force pilot. He was highly symptomatic: agitated, abusing prescription drugs, depressed, behaving in ways that were out of character for him. What I knew going into the first session was that he'd recently lost six buddies in a helicopter accident in Afghanistan. Recall also that early in that session, as we discussed an unrelated topic, he blurted out that he'd been sexually abused at age nine, forced into sex with a babysitter.

Mindful of how early we were in our working relationship, I was concerned about the very issue we've been discussing in this chapter: too much, too soon. Yet, I was also aware that trauma survivors can so easily feel shut down, their past dismissed. I was conscious of his wish to share.

As I've been saying, for such clients, the therapist needs to provide a sense of containment. For people with histories of trauma, the past feels unwieldy, secrets seem explosive. How do we help pace the therapy? How do we slow things down to make the whole process more manageable?

Honor the Telling

The story is one thing, but the telling of the story is another. By focusing on the person's *relationship to* their own story, it's possible to honor the telling without explicitly encouraging a "give me the gory details" approach. Asking them, for example, if this was *the first time they've shared this with anyone? If so, what does it mean* to them, having told me—someone they really don't know just yet—an important secret about them? *What are they feeling right now, having shared this?* When traumatic experiences are disclosed too early, we see the person feeling exposed, vulnerable.

When I asked the pilot directly, he told me it felt "crappy." And I responded with appreciation for his honesty. With that, the two of us—therapist and client—now knew we shared something: knowledge that there was a deeply personal story in the client's life and that his story was a big deal. To honor the telling is to convey an awareness of its magnitude, as in, *I imagine this is something that's had a big impact on your life.* That's not so obvious when you've spent a lifetime trying to shut out your own past.

Honoring the telling also means conveying a sense of responsibility. Having blurted out what he did, the pilot entrusted me with his secret; the operative word being *me.* Other than his high school girlfriend, no one else knew. With that, I assumed a responsibility, and I let him know I understood it. Working with him in therapy, I took on the responsibility of helping him make sense of his history—no small task.

Flag the Topic for Therapy

The hurry to share comes from a wish to purge one's past, a fantasy that simply telling will fix everything. But why the need to rush headlong into it, why the urgency?

Put simply, secrecy is a burden. Yes, it's sometimes necessary, but having carried the burden for so long, the fear is, *If I don't tell now, it'll be too late, maybe I never will;* and the feeling is, *I need to get rid of my vile past, it's making me sick.*

To *flag* the topic for therapy is to slow everything down. Rather than trying to talk about a complex past quickly before the impulse to change one's mind, we move gradually. As if to say, your trauma history is important, we'll address this, but in good time. *Let's flag this as something we'll explore together, it'll be part of our work here.*

Although the air force pilot announced that he'd been sexually abused by his babysitter at age nine, I worked with him to slow the process down. In such cases, an apt metaphor used by my wife, psychiatrist Diane Philipp, is to *engage the low burner.* The story is right here in plain view, we can see it simmering— but let's hold off on a rolling boil *just yet.*

Revisit the Topic Soon

Having already honored the telling, and having flagged the person's traumatic past as a topic therapist and client will explore together, it's important *not* to let weeks and weeks pass before revisiting the matter. The clinician should bring it up again, soon.

Why is this important? Because the client doesn't know what's on the therapist's mind. It's so easy for people to let their fears get the better of them, for clients to imagine the therapist either isn't really interested or can't tolerate the traumatic part of the person's life, for them to worry: *Maybe I'm just too much for my therapist to handle.*

When people share their trauma history, it's taxing on their psychological resources. They've taken a huge emotional risk, sometimes feeling frightened by what they did, with no idea how the therapist will respond. Many already blame themselves for what happened to them, thinking they got what they deserved. Some imagine they brought it on themselves, perhaps by not fighting back. They view themselves as an imposition or as unworthy of help. They judge themselves harshly, just as they fear the judgment of others. They worry they won't be good parents, just as they've been hurt by those closest to them.

And now, here they are, having disclosed parts of their traumatic past . . . there's the possibility of feeling humiliated, exposed, foolish.

So when the therapist *comes back* to the person's story, that's reassuring to clients, it's containing. It communicates that the topic is of interest to the therapist, that the disclosure is indeed important. It conveys that the therapist isn't too uncomfortable or frightened to face this aspect of the person's history. In short, it assures: *This trauma of yours isn't bigger than the both of us.*

With the air force pilot, after he divulged a history of sexual abuse by his babysitter, as I mentioned above, I *honored* the telling, focusing on his feelings about having shared this with me. I then *flagged* it as an important topic that we'll unpack together over the upcoming weeks. And then, I inquired about other areas of his life: his relationship with his daughter, his feelings about his wife, his fear of messing up his military career, his newfound interest in religion, and so on. And then, toward the end of the session, I very briefly listed each of these as possible areas we can work on together, *including* the sexual abuse.

In other words, I brought the disclosure *back into the room*. I named the sexual abuse—I didn't go into explicit details, just named it, as if to say: It's truly an issue, here it is. I can see it, and you can see it. It's not all of your story, but it's part of your story. And together, we'll address it, in good time.

In this way, as therapists, we can help clients slow down their disclosures, giving time for painful stories to be shared more gradually, pacing the process, granting space to forge a therapeutic relationship, without overwhelming the person.

When the Therapist Rushes In

In *Trauma and Recovery* (1992), Judith Herman wrote about the potential for therapeutic missteps when working with trauma survivors. She noted with great concern: "Programs that promote the rapid uncovering of traumatic memories without providing an adequate context for integration are therapeutically irresponsible and potentially dangerous, for they leave the patient without the resources to cope with the memories uncovered" (p. 184).

Let's return to the case of David Morris. Recall that as a marine infantry officer, he was nearly killed on several occasions—once by an IED—in southern Baghdad in 2007. Years later, suffering from symptoms of PTSD, he was triggered in a movie theater due to an on-screen explosion. And he went to the San Diego VA hospital for therapy, where treatment soon went awry.

In his painstaking account *The Evil Hours* (2015), Morris certainly portrays the therapist as naïve and inexperienced. And while it comes across loud and clear that, for the client, there was no sense of containment, no feeling of confidence in the therapeutic relationship before being asked to detail the trauma, what also comes across is how *earnest* the young clinician was.

In fact, as Morris explained, the therapist tried to push the treatment right to the unfortunate end, even citing research to back up his claims: "We've had hundreds, even thousands of veterans go through this, and it worked for them," the clinician said (2015b, p. 194).

What does it matter if he was earnest? When therapists rush into trauma details, without providing adequate preparation, it's usually with the best of intentions. In my years of supervising in the field, I've seen clinicians vary widely in skill level, in readiness for the work, in personal maturity, and so on. But I've rarely seen trauma therapists who weren't committed—often deeply so—to helping others.

It's precisely from a place of commitment, from an intent to help those who are troubled, that we see aspirations to *fix* the client, and to do so quickly. Not that I have anything against people feeling better . . . don't we *want* to end suffering? But, when therapists come at the trauma, guns blazing, without the kind of patience necessary to build basic trust, without fostering safety first, without forging containment in the therapeutic relationship, what we have is an enactment of the *rescue fantasy*.

Beware the Quick Fix

It's painful to see people suffer. We want to "fix" the suffering, to make it go away. We want to rescue those in great emotional turmoil. And especially when clients themselves express distress at their posttraumatic symptoms, there's every reason to feel compelled to help speedily.

But the fix isn't quick. In trauma work especially, the therapeutic relationship takes time to develop. As I pointed out in *Trauma and the Avoidant Client* (2010), "There can be felt pressure on the clinician to act, to try excessively to make things better. When such a sentiment is strong, the therapist can easily cross into the realm of acting on feelings, making attempts to manage personal, difficult emotions arising from the therapy by taking care of, and by taking-over. But in the process, the clinician may be undermining the treatment" (p. 118).

While the wish to end suffering is understandable—even admirable—there's also a certain self-serving aspect to trauma work, an aspect that fuels the rescue fantasy. Namely, trauma therapy *feels important*. Of course, it *is* important. Under the right treatment conditions, even those who've endured unspeakable suffering can find a way to live with their past, to recover, and, for many, to learn from their painful experiences.

But here, what I'm referring to is the *impression* of it being important, the sense—shared by therapist and client—that the stakes are high. People who have survived interpersonal trauma are often left symptomatic, struggling in relationships, carrying dark secrets, feeling insecure about themselves and their future. Even as they struggle to trust the therapist, the client may project onto the clinician a sense of importance. This feeling may be communicated unwittingly. Psychologist Constance Dalenberg explained: "As therapist and client discuss great adversity, the painful events can become a shared burden. The members of the dyad often become bonded through their (possibly secret or illicit) knowledge of the trauma and at times through their joint identification with this trauma" (2000, p. 202).

It's very easy for the clinician to get drawn into trying to rescue the person from their suffering, to relieve them quickly, because it *feels* important to do so. There's a shared sense that there are grave consequences here. Some clients even play a role in giving this impression: *This therapy is my last resort.* Or, taken one step further: *You're my last resort.*

This impression of importance can make it challenging for therapists to exercise patience in listening, to do the gradual work of building safety and trust in the treatment relationship, before unpacking traumatic experiences. And, returning to David Morris's case, when clinicians get drawn into frank attempts to *prove* to the client the importance of trauma therapy—*We've had hundreds, even thousands of veterans go through this, and it worked for them*—something in the therapist has been activated, as if shouting to the world, *Hey, this is really important work!*

Rather than preparing the client *for* that work, getting them ready by providing containment, by gradually forging trust in the relationship, by building a sense of safety to open up, the clinician is—as in James Chu's analogy—inviting the client to step off a rooftop.

When Therapists Export the Quick Fix

Many therapists have faced strong criticism for encouraging people to open up in the wrong context or without adequate preparation. Among mental health practice critics, journalist Ethan Watters has been particularly vocal. In a popular Berkeley Arts and Letters program interview (Mytinger & Madan, 2010), Watters laments how American trauma counselors have now taken it upon themselves to rush into other cultures after wars and natural disasters, with claims to having special knowledge about trauma and its effects on the human psyche.

Watters's great worry is that our understanding of trauma—indeed, our understanding of the mind—is tied to culturally specific ways of healing. And that by bringing therapists hastily into disaster zones, without an appreciation for cultural nuance, we may be missing important differences, and in the process doing more harm than good. In Watters's words: "We fail to understand what anthropologists know and what historians know, which is that reactions to trauma actually vary across cultures, and vary over times. It's not one thing. And different cultures have different meanings attached to not only the events, but the expectations for how the psychology will affect you. And those meanings matter a great deal" (Mytinger & Madan, 2010).

Concerned about the proliferation of American mental health paradigms across the world, Watters (2010) studied the aftermath of the December 2004 tsunami in Sri Lanka. And while his broad-brushstroke portrayal of trauma therapists is unapologetically two-dimensional—the field is made to look uniformly silly—his observations are nonetheless important.

Namely, there was a wholesale rush to "fix" the trauma as quickly as possible. "The longer we wait, the more the damage," explained a psychologist to the *Washington Post*.[1] Two weeks after the Christmas Day natural disaster that would drown over a quarter million people in Sri Lanka, hundreds of Western trauma counselors descended en masse to offer help. In Watters's description, few understood the languages spoken, the religious practices, local grieving and burial rituals, or the country's extensive history of civil war.

They had headed to Sri Lanka with almost no knowledge of the culture, and they acted quickly. Referring to the interventions as "assembly-line counseling" Watters wrote: "The pace of counseling often rivaled the speed of an emergency room. Over two four-day periods in late January and February, one organization reported giving psychotherapy and counseling to 1,724 people, including 631 children. This was an impressive feat given that they had only two dozen counselors to do the work" (2010, pp. 79–80).

As a science writer and journalist, Watters is unflinchingly critical of Western mental health therapies—both psychological and psychiatric—and of trauma therapy in particular. For those of us in the field who work with traumatized clients on a regular basis, such criticism can be hard to hear. And for therapists who, with good intention, made it their concern to help others across the world, for no compensation, it may seem all too easy to be the armchair critic. Still, Watters's concerns are valid and should be taken seriously if we're to honestly help survivors recover.

Trauma work takes time. There's no hurrying it along, no substitute for listening, patience, cultural nuance, and the gradual building of a safe, trusting relationship. When therapists rush in, they undermine the work and undermine recovery, making it harder for people to seek treatment down the road.

1. See Watters, 2010, p. 70.

The State of the Art: Phase-Based Trauma Therapy

A central theme is that when people are recovering from interpersonal trauma, it's important to give permission to take it one step at a time. Therapists can use the treatment relationship to pace the process of opening up. This chapter is about exercising restraint, about being measured in the therapeutic process. As Watters and others show us, it's remarkably easy for the intriguing aspects of traumatic events to draw the clinician in. How easy it is, then, to lose sight of the survivor's needs.

Clients require time in treatment to prepare for what is to be painful work. Therapists need to familiarize themselves with client cultural and family context, as well as client coping resources, before suggesting they undertake an emotionally grueling process. And the treatment relationship needs time to incubate.

What Does the Research Say?

To make the process much more manageable, treatment for relational trauma should follow a *phase-based* approach. James Chu (2011) describes the three stages of therapy:

1. Establishing safety, stabilization, control of symptoms, and overall improvement in ego functioning
2. Confronting, working through, and integrating traumatic memories
3. Continued integration, rehabilitation, and personal growth

Most phase-oriented trauma treatment follows this three-stage approach. The most comprehensive description is in Judith Herman's *Trauma and Recovery* (1992).

But more recently, several other leading trauma therapy innovators and researchers have come out in strong support of the method as well, including psychologists Christine Courtois (Courtois & Ford, 2013), Paul Frewen (Frewen & Lanius, 2015), Anna Baranowsky (Baranowsky & Gentry, 2015), and Marylene Cloitre (Cloitre, Cohen, & Koenen, 2006). Parenthetically, one of the earliest descriptions of phase-oriented trauma therapy dates back to the 1880s, in the work of French psychologist and neurologist Pierre Janet (see van der Hart, Brown, & van der Kolk, 1989).

In a description of the underpinnings of the phase-based approach, psychologist Christine Courtois referred to it as "a meta-model that encourages careful sequencing of therapeutic activities and tasks, with specific initial attention to the individual's safety and ability to regulate his or her emotional state. The treatment has a whole-person philosophy that does not overemphasize the traumatic antecedents of the individual's difficulties above all else, yet does give them appropriate emphasis and importance. Gold (2000) has labelled this strategy as 'not trauma alone'" (2008, p. 92).

To date, one of the most definitive studies on the phase-oriented approach was done by psychologist Marylene Cloitre and colleagues. Their 2010 *American Journal of Psychiatry* paper reports results of a randomized controlled trial of 104 women with PTSD related to childhood abuse—that is, women who'd experienced early-life and chronic traumatization. They found that phase-based treatment showed greater benefits and fewer adverse effects than the two comparison conditions, with improvement continuing well after therapy had ended.

In an investigation conducted under the auspices of the International Society for Traumatic Stress Studies (ISTSS) that surveyed the opinions of trauma treatment experts, Cloitre et al. (2011) found that the majority of respondents endorsed phase-oriented therapy for complex trauma.[2] In their expert consensus treatment guidelines, the ISTSS concludes that "the use of a phase-based treatment approach for adults with Complex PTSD has excellent consensus" (Cloitre et al., 2012, p. 12).

Maggie Revisited

Let's see how a phase-oriented approach looks in practice. In Chapter 1, I describe treatment with Maggie, a young mother I worked with several years ago.

---

2. Complex trauma is defined in the ISTSS expert survey as typically of an interpersonal nature, occurring under circumstances where escape is not possible due to physical, psychological, maturational, environmental, or social constraints. The most common examples are childhood sexual and physical abuse, but it also includes domestic violence, sex trafficking, and others. Symptoms tend to fall into five broad domains: emotion regulation difficulties, disturbances in relational capacities, alterations in attention and consciousness (e.g., dissociation), adversely affected belief systems, and somatic distress or disorganization.

Because Maggie had refused a routine pelvic exam, her family doctor referred her to me, suspecting a history of prior sexual abuse. Her weight was very low, and she met criteria for depression. Early on, she and I mostly sat in silence. I worried I wasn't being helpful at all, but she was attending sessions regularly, and we had reasonable rapport. She even expressed concern when I said I'd be away because of a conference, so it seemed that therapy was beginning to matter to her.

But other than a brief disclosure in one of our first sessions, I didn't know much about her past, until she started e-mailing me about her disturbing history as a child. At the age of eight, her fourteen-year-old brother would sexually abuse her, threatening her if she didn't keep it all quiet.

Maggie's case is a good example of active phase-based trauma treatment, for someone with a history of early relational abuse.

We worked together in stages, first focusing on her feelings of safety, gradually building the therapeutic relationship before getting too far into her trauma history. As I describe in Chapter 1, early in the work, Maggie spontaneously sent me e-mails with disturbing, traumatic stories from her past. I would honor these in session, flag them as topics to come back to, and come back to them in later sessions, as she became more ready. I also instructed her on deep breathing and grounding skills. These would be helpful later, when we'd discuss her past more specifically. We also worked actively on helping her notice and understand personal triggers and the feelings they provoked. In this first phase, we worked on helping her stabilize her dangerously low weight and mood, and to that end, some sessions included her husband.

Only after building a greater sense of safety did we concentrate on unpacking traumatic memories and feelings and on reflecting on the meaning of those experiences in her life. In this second phase (as I describe in Chapter 1), we put together a trauma narrative, where she'd discuss her traumatic experiences and consider their implications. She would become visibly anxious reliving the particulars. And at those times, I'd help her slow her breathing and remind her of her grounding techniques—for example, asking her to rub her hands together and other sensory experiences—to bring her back to the present, where it was safe. After this, we would continue focusing on her traumatic stories.

She reached a point where she could better tolerate painful emotions; she could sit with vulnerable feelings alongside someone she could trust and increasingly face the truth of her traumatic history and what it meant to her, without becoming so overwhelmed. By then, she was no longer elusive when referring to the trauma, or afraid to mention her brother's name. Instead, she would notice traumatic memories as they arose, feeling them, owning them . . . recognizing them as painful aspects of her past, but not letting them consume or define her.

The third and final stage of trauma therapy is often labeled *reconnection*, as there's a shift toward better connection with others and improved connection with parts of the self. There are also greater feelings of empowerment in relationships and personal growth. With Maggie, this stage of treatment focused a lot on her role as a mother and how that fit into her personal identity: her sense of responsibility for her family, her fear that she wouldn't be able to adequately protect her child—as she had often felt unprotected—and how difficult it still was for her to stand up for herself.

In the next chapter, we examine more specifically how *safety* is cultivated. As we've been exploring, early in the work, clients need a sense of containment. And they need to feel more stable within themselves before unpacking traumatic experiences, feelings, and relationships. Chapter 5 looks further at how we foster a safe therapeutic space.

Cultivating Safety Within a Relational Framework

The Case of Robin

For months, Robin had tried to tough it out. As a body builder, that was easy to do. Adding more workouts to her usual routine, she could keep herself busy. There was the gym where she normally trained, two hours daily, before starting work as an information systems technician. And, for the past three months, Robin had spent her lunch hour at the company's fitness center as well. But when she began adding workouts at her condo unit too, sometimes lasting through the evening, her partner, Lyndsay, began to worry.

The original contact for therapy came by e-mail. And following a couple of exchanges with Robin, including confirmation of time and place, I soon found—to my surprise—that I was seated face to face with the *two of them* in my office. (Based on the e-mail exchange, I'd imagined seeing Robin alone.)

But Lyndsay was worried about her girlfriend. She wanted her back to normal. And she wanted to be part of the solution. Doing most of the talking, she explained about the overexercising. The weekend prior, unable to find her anywhere in the unit, Lyndsay went down to the gym, where she found Robin on the elliptical machine, at 3 a.m.

Lyndsay also told me about the restless legs, explaining that for months now, in bed, she couldn't get Robin to stop moving. "So I've managed to wean her off caffeine," she elaborated brightly.

But the worst part was the nightmares. Robin had virtually the same dream over and over again. She couldn't stand it anymore. She didn't want to go to bed—she was *terrified* of going to bed.

The dream: Marcus their dog, a brown and white shih tzu, is alive again and can be found somewhere in their tenth-floor condo unit. Sometimes he's in the bedroom, sometimes on the porch. He plays, and all is well. But soon, he "pisses and shits" on the floor. And Robin, angered by this, sticks his face in it—hard!—somehow hurting him in the process. Now, in the veterinarian's office, she hears the news: Marcus has terminal cancer. He'll be dead within two weeks.

Marcus was real. And soon I'd discover that much of the dream had matched Robin's lived experience—it was a constant revisiting of her recent past. Having died six months earlier from terminal cancer, Marcus had lost bladder and bowel control toward the end, sometimes frustrating Robin, who did indeed lash out at him on occasion, much to her regret. She felt humiliated, ashamed of herself.

The nightmares were torture. Robin was both terrified and plagued by her own self-loathing, from which the nightmares would give no respite.

And Lyndsay could no longer bear to see Robin like this. Trying to help, she'd say what she could. In the following brief exchange toward the end of the first session, Lyndsay attempts to somehow alleviate her girlfriend's suffering. She tries to use reassurance:

Lyndsay: "But he was old, okay? I mean really old, like seriously, what else could you have done for him? Old dogs die, okay?"

Robin looks down at her feet, says nothing.

Lyndsay (turning toward me): "I don't know what to do with her, Dr. Muller. It's like she *wants* to be miserable. I mean, it's been six months. I didn't get that upset when my own *sister* died. And this was a dog. I mean, seriously. A dog!"

Lyndsay turns back toward Robin, who has buried her face in her hands. Lyndsay's demeanor softens as she reaches toward her girlfriend, gently running her hand through Robin's short, blond-highlighted hair. She leans in to kiss her on the forehead.

Robin looks up at her, as Lyndsay pronounces, almost in a whisper, "I just want you normal. Okay? Let's make you normal again. I want you to be happy again, baby." And then Lyndsay looks in my direction, as if reading my reaction or, perhaps, seeking my approval.

Taking the Client's Suffering Seriously: A Stance That Brings Safety to the Therapeutic Relationship

At this point, we don't *really* know what's going on. What we do know is that Robin feels an overwhelming loss in the death of her beloved pet. Why her feelings are so profound, why she's tormented by nightmares and agitation, why we see symptoms of depression—that's all unclear as of yet.

We're also curious about Robin's sense of humiliation and shame. She hates herself for those moments of intolerance and feelings of aggression toward Marcus. She can't forgive herself. And until she can understand—and accept—her interactions with Marcus when he was alive, she won't let go of him in death. This is often the case with unresolved grief.

And, there's her relationship with Lyndsay. Kindhearted and sweet, Lyndsay certainly means well. Like so many who struggle with depression in loved ones, she wants, more than anything, to "fix" Robin. But her impatience lies just below the surface. Lyndsay wants her strong-minded girlfriend back to normal, and she feels at a loss, not knowing what to do with *this* version of Robin. Lyndsay is gentle with her, yes, but there's an element of "performance" in the interaction. She's performing in the role of supportive girlfriend, but her patience is starting to wear thin.

On some level, it seems, Robin picks up on the expectation to "get over it already." The extent of her guilt, her regret, her self-loathing . . . all in the wake of Marcus's death, makes no sense to her, or to others in her life. So she shuts up about it, and instead overexercises, as a kind of drug, to distract and to numb the pain.

Some losses are hard to take seriously. When we talk about the *overwhelming* aspect of trauma, difficulty adjusting to so-called overwhelming life experiences, what the concept misses is the subjective nature of "overwhelming:" One person's stress is another's trauma.

And yes, naturally, there are norms anchoring us to what is outside the realm of usual human experience. All the examples discussed in the book would be widely regarded as interpersonally traumatic. But what's compelling about Robin's early presentation in treatment is that it's not so clear-cut.

Unlike sexual or physical abuse, parental abandonment, domestic abuse, rape, and violent death, it's hard to know *how* to regard *some* painful life experiences: death of a pet, miscarriage of pregnancy, job loss . . . it can be so easy to minimize their impact. When we don't feel "justified" in our distress, when we tell ourselves the experience doesn't "count" as traumatic, when the suffering somehow doesn't seem warranted—and yet we suffer—it's a challenge to know how to make sense of it all. And it leaves us wondering, why are we experiencing *this* as so overwhelming?

In psychotherapy, in trauma therapy in particular, it's easy to focus on the traumas that "count" and miss the ones that "don't"—as defined by . . . well . . . us. As if only *certain* suffering is licensed. As if the others may, just as easily, be dismissed. Our preconceived, culturally embedded notions about trauma color our understanding. And for us therapists, they influence what we target in psychotherapy. They tell us what to take seriously.

And especially when clients struggle with the exact same thing . . . how to take their own painful experiences seriously, how to accept the legitimacy of their distress, how to refrain from comparing their suffering to others', therapist and client can collude to miss the obvious.

That's precisely what happened in my work with Robin. Early on, she struggled to take her *own* reactions to Marcus's death seriously, sometimes repeating, in utter frustration with herself, *but he was only a dog!*

But he was only a dog . . . is this really something one takes seriously?

Robin's Backstory

The second session was with Robin alone. And it was interesting to see that, without her girlfriend there, she came across differently. In the first couple of chapters, I describe the Adult Attachment Interview (AAI), a psychological procedure that assesses the person's relational state of mind: their understanding of attachment, how they think about their interpersonal world (George et al., 1996; Hesse, 1999; Steele & Steele, 2008). The method orients the client to think about their early experiences with caregivers.

That second meeting was an AAI. Early in the interview, clients are asked to list five adjectives describing their childhood relationship with a given caregiver, going back as far as they remember. And then they're asked to go through the adjectives one at a time. Although challenging, they're invited to recall specific incidents or examples from their personal history. What we learn from the process is how clients make *sense* of their remembered story, how they make meaning of it.

Robin was an only child, and her parents decided to separate when she was eleven. From that moment onward, as she explained, her parents made each other's lives a living hell. She moved with her mom to a poor, working-class neighborhood, while her father retained the upscale home they'd all lived in before the separation.

Always seemingly in control, her father took her mother to court, claiming parental alienation. A lawyer by profession, her father cross-examined Robin on the witness stand, putting words in her mouth and using her words against her, she said, statements she'd made innocently during weekend visits. Her mother, addicted to pain medication, would often "lose her shit," Robin told me, overreacting to one minor thing or another, such as low grades, messiness, or dirty dishes. And much of the time, she was emotionally absent.

But despite her father's irritating litigiousness, as a young child she'd always felt close to him—closer than she did to her mom. She recalled when she was young, seeking her dad during the night if she felt ill. And in grade school, when the boys relentlessly called her fat, and the girls teased her for being "uncoordinated," her father signed the two of them up for father-daughter karate classes.

In the middle of the night, during winter vacation—Robin was now about fifteen—she woke with a start, she'd heard a loud noise. It had come from her father's bedroom. As his door was locked and she couldn't get in, panic stricken, she called emergency services. Arriving within minutes, they soon broke down the door, keeping her out of the room. She was shuffled outside, where she waited for what felt like an eternity.

She never was allowed to witness the scene in vivo. But she found out, minutes later, that her worst fears were confirmed. As she'd slept soundly in her room, just down the hall, her father had shot himself. He was dead.

"Asshole!" Robin said, raising her voice, slapping her thigh. "What an asshole. He had to kill himself while I was visiting."

And yet, even as she relayed the story to me—the first time I was hearing it—she had some insight. "He was *using* me to piss my mom off. He manipulated me, to get to her. Why would he do that? Who *does* that? The selfish prick traumatized me to piss my mother off! . . . That's my father."

I understood from Robin's AAI that her anger came from betrayal: Her father was willing to abandon her, to spite her mother. And since then, Robin had been preoccupied by hurt and rage. The suicide of her father remained an unresolved traumatic loss. In her anguish, in her fury, she was keeping him alive.

When the *Therapist* Struggles to Take the Suffering Seriously

So, how does the dog fit in?

This is where *I* enter the picture. As therapists, we constantly make choices about where to intervene, what to focus on, what to take seriously. As I said earlier, in trauma therapy it's easy to focus on the traumas that, from our perspective, "count," as if there were some clear-cut hierarchy of suffering.

And I must confess, my own bias—I've never particularly been a "dog person"—played into this as well. When I heard the story of her father's suicide, when I saw Robin's continued hurt and rage, I understood it as an unresolved traumatic loss. And I experienced an immediate "Aha!" inside, as if I were saying to myself, "So *that's* what all this dog grief is about . . . it's really about her *father!*"

Now, I'm not saying I did this in any obvious, clumsy way. I wasn't insensitive or dismissive. It's more that, for me, as a listener, hearing about her father's suicide touched me personally, in a way that the death of Marcus hadn't. When I worked with Robin, my own children were teenagers, and imagining her as a fifteen-year-old kid, panic stricken, desperately hoping her father was alright, only to find out—in the cruelest of ways—he wasn't . . . I immediately felt a personal connection to *that* story.

As for the dog? Not so much.

My bias, subtle as it was, colored our work together for the next few months. When Marcus came up, it wasn't that I showed particular insensitivity, it was more that I just wasn't giving her what she needed. An authentic empathy perhaps? I'm not sure what, but I kept missing the mark.

As for Robin, she was quite literally hearing from friends, from Lyndsay, from her mother: *But he was only a dog!* Which she would say to herself as well, concluding, *I shouldn't be this upset!* The dismissiveness she heard from others only fueled her shame, her misguided conviction: There was something wrong with her for feeling as she did.

About three months into our work together, something shifted. A close friend of mine lost her father. Jewish, like me, she observed the custom of sitting shiva, seven days of ritual mourning. With complete severance from normal daily activity, the mourner is expected to sit with the loss, think about it, fully embrace it, although in practice the custom varies widely. Usually, there's a lot of prayer, ritual, and of course food.

A few days into the shiva of my friend's father, I realized that Robin had never sat shiva for her dog. That's what she needed.

And no, Robin wasn't Jewish. What I realized had more to do with me. What shifted was my way of *understanding* Robin. I needed to help her grieve the loss of Marcus authentically, without judgment. I needed to set aside my biases and sit alongside her as she reviewed Marcus's life.

I asked her to bring in photographs, to describe personal moments, anecdotes both happy and sad. I invited her to share her journal entries, of which there were many, from Marcus's last few days. I treated the loss no differently than the death of any loved one. I wondered with her if there was anything she still wanted Marcus to know, what had been left unsaid; what would she apologize to him for? In short, I understood his death as a big deal, because it *was* a big deal, in its own right, *to her*.

I knew something profound had changed in her when she announced one session that over the weekend she had planted a commemorative tree in Marcus's memory, in the dog park near their condo. Yes, she felt sad planting it, but she also felt joy.

And while the focus of treatment did eventually shift to the traumatic loss of her father, *that* work couldn't have happened just a few months earlier. Only once she was able to grieve the loss of her dog could she begin grieving the loss of her father.

I had to take her subjective experience seriously. I had to meet her where she was at, for her to feel safe enough to open up. Only once we take the client's suffering seriously do we bring safety to the therapeutic relationship. This is fundamental to trauma therapy.

Naming and Validating Traumatic Experiences: A Practice That Brings Safety to the Therapeutic Relationship

To take suffering seriously, it's important to name it. Let's look at this idea, as considered by Ifemelu, the protagonist in *Americanah* (2014), a fictional account by novelist Chimamanda Ngozi Adichie; it's the story of a young Nigerian woman, a college student who had recently immigrated to the United States. The character struggles to find her footing and becomes disillusioned along the way. Adichie wrote:

> Ginika said: "I think you're suffering from depression." Ifemelu shook her head and turned to the window. Depression was what happened to Americans, with their self-absolving need to turn everything into an illness. She was not suffering from depression; she was merely a little tired and a little slow. "I don't have depression," she said. Years later, she would blog about this: "On the Subject of Non-American Blacks Suffering from Illnesses Whose Names They Refuse to Know." A Congolese woman wrote a long comment in response: She had moved to Virginia from Kinshasa and, months into her first semester of college, begun to feel dizzy in the morning, her heart pounding as though in flight from her, her stomach fraught with nausea, her fingers tingling. She went to see a doctor. And even though she checked "yes" to all the symptoms on the card the doctor gave her, she refused to accept the diagnosis of panic attacks because panic attacks happened only to Americans. Nobody in Kinshasa had panic attacks. It was not even that it was called by another name, it was simply not called at all. Did things begin to exist only when they were named? . . . We don't talk about things like depression in Nigeria, but it's real. (pp. 194–195)

Although the author focuses here on naming the "depression," the character's symptoms follow a period of shame and sexual trauma, which occurred in the scene just before. Without getting bogged down in specific diagnosis, the point is still well taken: Naming the suffering gives it character, makes it real.

And naming traumatic experiences takes them seriously. In short, it *validates* them.

How Naming Traumatic Experiences Brings Validation

Survivors of interpersonal trauma—especially trauma within the family—have often grown up in *invalidating environments*. In psychologist Marsha Linehan's (1993) view, invalidation undermines individuals' understanding of their own experiences, their self-knowledge. It makes them doubt their interpretations of their own motivations and actions.

In the family of origin, the person's feelings are disregarded, leaving them unable to recognize or bear their own emotions (Rizvi, Steffel, & Carson-Wong, 2013). In such homes, when they do share private experiences, their feelings are minimized, dismissed. They're met with criticism or punishment. From an environment like this, people misunderstand what they've been through. They're left confused about who they are.

Psychologist Pamela Alexander (2015) finds that invalidating environments are prevalent in cases of child abuse and are even more common in cases of neglect. Linehan (1993) described the issue well:

> Sexual abuse, as it occurs in our culture, is perhaps one of the clearest examples of extreme invalidation during childhood. In the typical case scenario of sexual abuse, the victim is told that the molestation or intercourse is "Ok" but that she must not tell anyone else. The abuse is seldom acknowledged by other family members, and if the child reports the abuse she risks being disbelieved or blamed. . . . Similarly physical abuse is often presented to the child as an act of love or is otherwise normalized by the abusive adult. (pp. 53–54)

Invalidating environments are confusing. They make people second guess their own memories, doubting what they know to be true, disregarding themselves. They're left discounting their own traumatic experiences, mistrusting their own self-knowledge, wondering: Did that *really* happen to me? And if it wasn't such a big deal, why am I *feeling* like it was? What's *wrong* with me?

When we name traumatic experiences for what they are, we validate them. We convey to clients that what they went through, what they lost, what they suffered . . . that was real. It can't and shouldn't be ignored or trivialized. Unless we validate the person's experience, those who have suffered feel no safety in our presence.

This is, in part, why I support the use of *trigger warnings* on university campuses, why I include them, where relevant, in my own courses. In a 2015 *New York Times* opinion piece, philosophy professor Kate Manne described her reasons for adopting them, explaining that the practice originated in internet communities to benefit people with posttraumatic stress disorder (PTSD), to flag content, to give choice on whether to read on. And that in university settings, professors who use them give students notice in syllabi or before certain reading assignments. People can prepare themselves for material they're about to engage with, to better manage their reactions. Manne emphasized that students are still expected to attend and participate.

And while journalists and free-speech advocates alike worry the practice will shut down discussion of difficult material (Lukianoff & Haidt, 2015; Shulevitz, 2015), I've found that, when used judiciously, precisely the opposite is true: rather than shutting down discussion, students become even more engaged. In my graduate trauma therapy course, from time to time I assign the novel *Push* (Sapphire, 1996) on which the well-known 2009 film *Precious* was based. With its haunting depiction of intrafamilial rape and violence, the title is listed on my syllabus with a trigger warning. Yes, some students get triggered, and yes, they still show up to discuss the material, in earnest.[1]

Trigger warnings pay attention to people who so often are ignored. They underscore, within the broader social context, that PTSD really exists. Traumatized people exist. No, survivors needn't be "coddled," so to speak. But trauma can be tenacious.

In the naming, we validate. And in the naming, we highlight how histories have their consequences. Naming trauma is an act of truth-telling. It's necessary for survivors to understand why they feel as they do. It facilitates healing. It cultivates safety in the therapeutic relationship.

Clients Don't Accept Validation So Readily

In practice, naming client traumatic experiences for what they are—validating them—can be quite the challenge. Why? Because, clients often invalidate their *own* traumatic histories.

---

1. On rare occasion, when students have found material too emotionally stirring to discuss in class, they opt instead to write a brief paper on the topic.

In Chapter 2, I talk about how trauma brings self-deception. When I was a graduate student in the late 1980s, psychologists Audrey Berger and John Knutson discovered a self-deception phenomenon I still find astonishing (Berger, Knutson, Mehm, & Perkins, 1988). In a nonclinical sample, the authors initially asked people about their parents' disciplinary practices, along with specifics: Did their parents use objects punitively? Were injuries sustained? Was medical attention required? And so on. These questions were framed neutrally, behaviorally—the words *trauma* and *abuse* weren't used, just yet. But then afterward, once participants had given a detailed behavioral account, they were asked to reflect on what turned out to be a really tough question: whether they'd ever been *physically abused* by their parents as a child.

Replicating the study four times before publishing the results, the authors found that only a fraction (27 percent) of those who reported violent parenting practices—including the identification of specific injuries sustained—ended up actually *labeling* themselves as having experienced physical abuse. The results were not subtle. Even among those reporting that parental discipline led to broken bones, dental injuries, head injuries, and burns, only a *minority* (roughly 40 percent) classified themselves as having been physically abused.

In a replication of these findings on a clinical sample, the authors studied physically abused teenagers receiving help from a local department of social services (Berger et al., 1988). They found very similar results: Fewer than 20 percent of these adolescents—who'd been physically and sexually abused (defined by objective criteria)—said they'd experienced "abuse" from their parents.

As noted in Chapter 2, I describe the self-deception that goes with trauma. Here, I'd like to underscore that naming traumatic experiences, validating them, is easier said than done. For so many, there's something very uncomfortable about applying terms like *trauma* or *abuse* to themselves.

When people dismiss or minimize the magnitude of their own anguish, they invalidate their past. We see this often. Clients with even the most horrendous histories feel guilty for coming to therapy with such "minor problems," worrying they're wasting my precious time, worrying they're "whining"—as if, on some hierarchy of suffering, theirs doesn't count. *You should be seeing someone with real problems.*

We see this *self-invalidation* when clients feel undeserving of therapy, unworthy of help. *Shouldn't I just figure this out for myself?* And we see it when they justify the past, saying they deserved what they got, they somehow brought it on themselves, it was their own fault. *I didn't fight back enough, I was weak.*

At the age of nine, Tony Rodgers was raped by a man. As an adult, he recollects the aftermath of the abuse. In the film *Boys and Men Healing From Child Sexual Abuse* (Barbini & Weinberg, 2010), Rodgers explained:

> So when they caught the guy, and they brought him to trial, it was after my tenth birthday, and shortly after the trial was done, my dad left. So I felt like he left because he had a son who couldn't defend himself. My father had taught me to fight, he taught me to box, and play football. And then he just left. So I felt like he left because I was weak. It was true . . . I always thought that asking for help would make me appear to be weak, or not man enough.

We see self-invalidation when clients struggle with the term *victim*, finding the word itself weak, pathetic. I've referred to this in previous work (Muller, 2009) as the *I'm-no-victim* identity, where some trauma survivors disconnect themselves from the very *idea* of "victim."

For some, acknowledging their own past, seeing their suffering for what it was, identifying with *victim*, *trauma*, or *abuse* is just too painful. It frightens them, it makes them feel vulnerable.

Naming and Validating Client Traumatic Experiences: A Therapeutic Process

How, then, in practice do therapists name and validate client traumatic experiences?

At the client's pace. This is especially true early in therapy. When we're still cultivating a sense of safety, it's important for the clinician to adopt a balanced approach. Naming traumatic experiences for what they are, acknowledging what the client went through . . . that's important, yes. But it has to occur *at a pace the client can handle.*

In Chapter 2, I describe how people have mixed feelings about acknowledging their traumatic experiences. They want to share their painful stories, yet they're afraid, so they avoid their traumatic experiences, feelings, and relationships. But they want to stay guarded only so much, for only so long. They cycle between testing the waters—perhaps letting the therapist in a bit—and then putting up their guard soon after, shutting discussion down, distancing themselves from close others or from vulnerable feelings.

Going at the client's pace means speaking truthfully, directly, but doing so in a way the client can bear. It means naming client traumatic experiences, but viewing this as an ongoing *therapeutic process*, an ongoing negotiation, one that develops over treatment, one that can't be rushed.

This kind of validation is something the client can come to accept, with greater ease, over the course of the work. It lands with greater frequency, in time, as the person comes to trust the therapist more.

From early in treatment, it's important for the therapist to *notice* if the client uses euphemistic language: "The thing that happened." Does the client struggle to speak plainly? To name the traumatic experience for what it was, to use transparent terms: *rape, died, sexual abuse?*[2]

To the extent that the person whitewashes their own experiences through vague or elusive language, this is something the therapist can notice aloud, can be curious about, can ask about (again, let me emphasize the importance of monitoring reactions—to work at the client's pace). Has the person always referred to the traumatic experience like that? I once worked with a woman who referred to the excruciating death of her husband as "the cancer deal."

In naming the trauma, I float trial balloons. The client euphemistically tells a story that cannot, in all honesty, be described as anything but rape. In the context of our discussion, in passing, simply, plainly, I use the word *rape*. The client may bristle at the sound of it. That's alright, the language is still new to the person. I notice the reaction, I'm curious about it. I invite them to consider the word: *How does that sound to you?* If uncomfortable, if it sounds strong, brutish . . . we examine that together.

In this way, I work with the client, *progressively*, to find honest language for their suffering, language that doesn't overwhelm, but doesn't minimize . . . language that rings true, relative to where they're at.

---

2. Some clients *do* use plain, direct language to describe the trauma, but *still* do so in a way that's self-invalidating, when they do so in a constricted, flippant, or cynical way—without connecting emotionally to the pain of their own words. For example, *Yeah, he'd rape me . . . that's how he got his jollies!* Here, the client can name the trauma, yet in doing so, they're still detached, having cut off vulnerable feelings. This avoidance of painful emotions still reflects a lack of internal felt safety. In Chapter 7, we look at the idea of helping clients reconnect with their vulnerable feelings—hurt, sadness, rejection—about their traumatic experiences.

There's no requirement that the client adopt *my* language. I only ask them to consider it. And, as I point out above, people want to stay guarded for only so long. This is what happened in my work with Robin.

Recall that when she started working with me, Robin was hearing from friends, from her partner Lyndsay, from her mother: *But he was only a dog!* Which she would say to herself as well, concluding, *I shouldn't be this upset!* The dismissiveness she heard from others fueled her shame. And she believed there was something terribly wrong with her for feeling as she did: *This isn't the end of the world. Why am I so upset about it?*

I didn't try to argue her out of that, or enlighten her. I didn't *explain* to her in some "teachy" way, we know this or that about traumatic loss. I didn't, from on high, try to *push* a trauma perspective on her, something she wasn't ready for yet.

What I did do—once *I* was able to see it—was meet her where she was at, focus on the loss of her dog as the death of a *loved one*, validate her profound sense of grief, her struggle to forgive herself . . . help her sit shiva, as it were, for Marcus.

This resonated for her. In so much of her life, her pain had been discounted. Therapy represented a place where she could feel different, where she could be heard, where her personal experience was validated. And in short order, she did indeed feel safe enough to open up.

Honesty Brings Safety to the Therapeutic Relationship

In *Trauma and Recovery* (1992), Judith Herman describes how trauma therapy requires the adoption of a particular moral stance, a kind of solidarity with the survivor. Referring to it as a *moral commitment to truth-telling*, the truth is seen as a goal we strive for and get closer to. In her words:

> Working with victimized people requires a committed moral stance. The therapist is called upon to bear witness to a crime. She must affirm a position of solidarity with the victim. This does not mean a simplistic notion that the victim can do no wrong; rather, it involves an understanding of the fundamental injustice of the traumatic experience and the need for a resolution that restores some sense of justice. This affirmation expresses itself in

the therapist's daily practice, in her language, and above all in her moral commitment to truth-telling, without evasion or disguise. (p. 135)

We've been talking about taking the client's suffering seriously, validating the person's experience, naming traumatic histories for what they are. All are fundamental to this kind of moral stance. And all speak to the idea that trauma therapy can't happen without honesty. Without it, clients can't feel safe. As therapists, we need to pay close attention to honesty in the therapeutic relationship.

In chapter 1, I describe the story told by psychotherapist Rachel Sopher (2015), the grandchild of a Holocaust survivor who'd kept silent about his past. The story of her grandfather's imprisonment in Auschwitz had been kept a secret from her until she was twelve. And although the Holocaust continued to cast a heavy pall on the family—muting celebrations, undermining closeness—Sopher came to recognize its influence on her only when her own psychotherapist, normally rather quiet, explicitly labeled the Holocaust a trauma, one that affected every life it touched.

Instead of softening the truth, her therapist answered with an honest *yes* when Sopher asked her: *Do you really think the trauma of the Holocaust impacted my family, impacted my life?* In her case, Sopher benefited from a therapist willing to be frank. And, of course, she herself seemed to be at a point in her life when, at least in part, she *wanted* to know the truth about her past.

A climate of honesty brings a sense of safety to the therapeutic relationship. For therapists and clients alike, intuitively, this makes sense. But it's not always so easy to put this into practice.

Sometimes honesty is a burden, sometimes it comes at a price. It can certainly be distressing or frightening to people, as in many of the examples discussed so far. But honesty can also feel downright annoying or inopportune, making everything more complicated for the client. And that can pull the therapist in competing directions.

The clinician can get co-opted into ongoing dishonesty, into secret keeping, as we see in the following case examples:

It's the end of the session. And wife marches off toward the elevator, racing to avoid a parking ticket below. As I hand husband the appointment card, standing in the doorway he asks me—under his breath—*If I told her I was having an affair, do you think she could handle it?* And then he rushes off, as she calls him to hurry up, leaving me holding the bag, so to speak—holding his ambivalence. Do I insist on honesty—and the relationship explodes—or do I collude with the husband, get drawn into some kind of illicit pact with him, making our next few couples sessions a sham?

Or, in a different case:

A mother I've been treating for PTSD and depression confesses she's been greatly exaggerating her symptoms to her psychiatrist. Why? That way, she explains, she's prescribed twice the Prozac she needs. She takes half and gives the rest to her depressed son. At age thirty-five, he still lives at home, refusing treatment. Every morning, she sprinkles pulverized Prozac and sugar on his corn flakes. *But don't tell him, or he'll kill me.* Again, my moral commitment to truth-telling is tested. How do I proceed . . . with honesty? At what price?

And when the therapist does insist on a climate of honesty, even though it's necessary in the long run, the client can still experience it, in the moment, as unfair, rigid, or even naïve, with unwelcome consequences:

An elderly woman I worked with a few years ago finally lost patience with me. She'd received my invoice, referring to payment for a missed session. She'd get no insurance coverage for that missed appointment, and she was annoyed. Couldn't I just fudge the dates, or call it a treatment session . . . really, was it "such a big to-do"? On a fixed income, the nonreimbursement would be costly to her.

But this was someone who grew up with scandal at every turn. As a young girl, when her father had suffered a traumatic brain injury and was hospitalized for half a year, her mother's boyfriend moved into their home, sometimes sleeping in the parents' bed. The children were sworn to secrecy, never breathing a word about it, especially upon Dad's return.

Yes, she was annoyed with me; she even canceled the next two sessions. But on her return, she described an argument she'd had with her husband. What kind of business was I running anyway, he complained, *Everyone rips off insurance companies!* And in response to her husband, to her surprise, she found herself *defending* me, telling him he can't tell her what to do, *who* she can talk to, or what she can talk about; she'd had *more* than enough of that as a kid. Maybe her therapist *was* an idiot . . . but at least he was going about it honestly!

In trauma therapy, I err on the side of honesty—doggedly so—and let the chips fall where they may. Without it, how can clients—who've had their trust violated—feel safe in the psychotherapy relationship?

At times, clients welcome the honesty . . . other times, not so much.

Of course, I *could have* done as she'd asked. It would have been easy. I could have simply gratified her, indulged her request that I defraud the insurance company. But to what end? Indeed, it would have been more of the same, a replication of other times she'd experienced lies and deceit, and there were many. Manipulation would have entered our relationship, undermining the work.

When the clinician responds by crossing a line, *even* when the client asked them to, safety leaves the therapeutic relationship. How can the person know the therapist won't cross another? How can you trust a trauma therapist who is deceptive?

Instead of indulging her request that I do something dishonest, we explored what it meant to her that I wouldn't. Yes, in part, she saw my honesty as a good thing, defending me to her husband, and yes, she decided to come back to therapy. But it was a struggle for her to return, and she still found my adherence to honesty very irritating.

Moments like these, conflicts in the relationship, can be *used* in the service of the therapy—they're grist for the mill. (I explore this more in Chapter 8.) With my elderly client, rather than meeting her request that I do something dishonest, we instead examined what it meant to her that I wouldn't. And we came to *understand* the meaning of this conflict; we used it as a therapeutic opportunity. What was the *most annoying* thing about my honesty, I wondered aloud. Yes, in small part, it was about the money—she and her husband were saving for a trip. But more so, it wasn't the money or the honesty as much as my *insistence*, as she saw it, on honesty. She found it rigid, as if I were "bossing her around, acting all high-and-mighty," *like a preacher or something.*

In fact, she'd grown up Pentecostal, and she and her husband had left the church years earlier, soon after their infant son had died, a sudden nighttime crib death while the family slept. She'd felt blamed for the death: her preacher, her mother—everyone except her doctor faulted her and her husband. And the two of them felt alone in the loss. In me, she experienced a familiar self-righteousness, and she didn't like it—it irked her, it made her feel judged.

And with that, the conversation had now shifted. Her struggle, really, wasn't with my honesty as with feeling shamed, humiliated, condescended to. In my adopting a position of honesty, she saw me as sanctimonious, as if I were somehow looking down on her, as if I were viewing her as *less than.* And between the two of us, we'd enacted a theme very familiar to her: So often she'd felt judged by others.

We talked about the role judgment had played in her life, what it meant to her, and what she *felt* in its presence, the judgments others had placed on her, and the ones she'd placed on herself.

And the most painful one of all . . . the one she couldn't forgive herself for. She'd never shared this with anyone, it was even hard for her to say. After all, it had secretly plagued her for years.

A burning question: *Was it my fault? Did my son die because of me?*

When Crisis Calls: Prioritizing Basic Safety Needs

For several years, I've been teaching an advanced psychotherapy course for students in the doctoral program at York University in Toronto. I get a lot of questions, and sometimes I get stumped. I've thought about this one on and off . . . it's a tricky issue that gets asked a lot.

How do you get someone to leave an abusive partner?

I don't have a simple answer. I don't think one exists, at least not with any degree of certainty. I've often sat on the sidelines though, with clients in abusive relationships. And that can feel excruciating, especially when the alternatives *seem* so clear: One person is obviously mistreating another, victimizing another. I imagine a better life for the person, if they could just let the relationship go. But the truth is, you can't "get" anyone to do anything.

So often, the issues are gendered. A woman remains stuck in a cycle of abuse/false-apology/abuse, for reasons that on the surface appear unclear. Financial need, outward appearances, and dependent children play an important role in the decision to stay. But the genders can be flipped as well, and I've seen cases of men—cloaked in shame—abused by their partners, keeping it secret from family and friends.

For therapists—indeed, for loved ones who care about these people—the temptation is to tell them what to do, as if I "know better," as if saying to them: The version of you that *I* imagine is better than the one you can imagine for yourself.

Certainly, the temptation to lecture them is understandable. It's hard to sit by idly, as our clients get hurt by people in their lives. But in addition to undermining self-determination, a big problem with a pushy, I-know-better approach to people in the throes of victimization is that it doesn't work. Trash-talking the abusive partner, *telling* the victim he or she must leave . . . we imagine this as helpful, but in fact, rather than leaving the partner, it may just as well be easier to leave the therapist.

So as clinicians, what's the alternative? As much as possible, we need to work on fundamentals of safety, conceived of broadly: physical and psychological health, basic family functioning, freedom from legal or financial bullying, freedom from sexual manipulation or exploitation, maintenance of financial basics. And we remain a support to the person, on the sidelines, challenging—not admonishing—them: *How does this or that choice fit with your stated goals?*

Working with people in the midst of abusive life situations can be difficult. It's important work. It can make a tremendous difference for people to know they have an ally, one to help them sustain less collateral damage during the crisis. In fact, the psychotherapeutic part can't begin, truly, until the traumatizing event has passed, until some stability has been established or restored.

Unless there's basic safety in people's lives, they can't start the painful process of self-reflection. They're not yet ready to examine what their traumatic history *means* to them. Their safety—and the protection of their family—must come first.

One client, whose ex-partner had been physically abusive when she was pregnant, remained stuck in a coercive, violent relationship. Having grown up poor, now working as a minimum-wage receptionist at a car dealership, she had limited income. Years earlier, when she first met him, he was a successful contractor, and she became consumed with a certainty that her life would finally turn around. She was hopeful . . . he would give her a family. That was all she ever wanted.

The rapes began when she was pregnant. They continued after the birth of the child. Every two weekends, he would visit her and their toddler daughter, and she desperately wished he would take the child to the park, read her stories, show interest in her. Instead, the toddler would play alone—once burning herself with matches—while my client was forced to have painful intercourse in the bedroom. And then he'd leave.

For a few months, our work focused on basic safety. She'd never enjoyed intercourse with him. It *was*, in fact, rape. That idea was new to her—it came as a surprise. I didn't trash-talk him, but I was honest: On a regular basis, she was forced into sex against her will. She was being raped. *This is not what love looks like.*

She was dependent on him for money. We discussed local options for single mothers with young children, of which there were several, and she turned out to be quite astute in finding resources, many through her church. Her child's safety became a focus as well. And in part, her willingness to set limits sexually with her ex came from a place of protectiveness for her child. She couldn't bear the thought of losing her daughter. And the close call—when the child almost burned herself—frightened her.

After several months of this work, her self-esteem improving all the while, she began investigating community college programs. She figured she could double her income if she had firm administrative skills.

And it was only after she'd sent in her applications that we began the more reflective work. At that point, her sleep had improved somewhat, and she looked a bit healthier. Frankly, she no longer looked terrified all the time.

In this way, we worked on the fundamentals of safety, to help her through the instability, and later, we shifted to psychotherapy, once the period of crisis had passed. At that point, her ex-boyfriend was no longer in her life. And she no longer feared *for* her life and the life of her daughter.

Building an Internal Sense of Safety

Triggered Without Warning

To understand *triggers* and their place in psychotherapy in general, and trauma therapy in particular, it's helpful to spend some time on the idea of *metaphor*.

A terrific article on the role of metaphor in treatment was written by psychiatrist Arnold Modell (2009), of the Boston Psychoanalytic Institute. He described metaphor as the transfer of meaning from one context to another or from one domain to another. Modell emphasized how normally this kind of transfer is psychologically healthy. It's playful, it's imaginative.

We see this vividly in the metaphor, *All the world's a stage, and all the men and women merely players.* On one hand, it celebrates: everyday life elevated to a glorious theatrical production. On the other hand, it saddens: the glory of life reduced to a mere theatrical production. Metaphor can be transformative, creating similarities and differences in meaning that enrich memory and experience.

But a very different process happens in trauma. Here, the transfer of meaning becomes frozen, invariant, as a rigid connection between past and present (Modell, 2009). And it appears without warning—it can be automatic.

When we talk about *triggers*, we mean an *abrupt* connection to traumatic feelings, memories, or experiences. It's often involuntary: There's a sudden link to some other time or place, without really knowing why, or why it would be happening now. And there's a sense of familiarity. *I'm feeling unsafe* can be an impression the person has had before, a transfer from past to present, also without knowing why, or why *now*.

Sometimes triggers happen in obvious ways, where strong feelings can be "right there." Fear, rejection, abandonment can come up rapidly, and they can overwhelm. But triggers can be subtle too, where only in hindsight do we piece together an understanding.

One survivor, for example, who'd done a lot of work to improve her self-esteem, to build her workplace confidence, found herself feeling intimidated by a particular customer at work one day, later that evening noticing her clothing stank from perspiration. Once a common occurrence for her, to feel intimidated and to perspire, it was an anxious pattern that hadn't been around for a while. What was it about *this* customer's appearance, his manner, the interaction with him that triggered her *now*? What feelings had surfaced for her in his presence, and how were those feelings familiar or different? These were questions we explored together.

Triggers can also be highly personal, idiosyncratic. The connection from past to present can be a peculiar one, specific to the client.

Edmund Metatawabin, a First Nations (native Canadian) chief and writer, had been a child at the notorious St. Anne's residential school in Fort Albany, Ontario. Federally funded, the institution was responsible for horrific abuse, which, remarkably, included an electrified chair used to physically shock the children (Talaga, 2016). Even recently, almost sixty years after Metatawabin first started at the school, everyday sights and sounds can trigger old memories. In a Canadian Broadcasting Corporation interview, he explained: "This brings something into my stomach, it's involuntary. It jolts your body. I'm sensitive to high heels clipping on the floor, because you'd hear that clip, clip, clip, clip—fast walk, clip, clip, clip—before you'd get attacked by the supervisor" (Kelley & Bloch, 2015).

In my own practice, I've seen how unique triggers can be. One young woman I was treating, when I consulted at a university clinic in Toronto, got triggered at her chiropractor's office. It was the middle of winter, and they'd placed a "remove wet boots" sign at the entrance and, next to it, a mat for the placement of snow-covered items. Strong willed, often finding herself in conflict with others, she'd been working with me since school started in September. Identifying her triggers was part of what we'd been focusing on.

Within moments of arriving at her session, she announced to me, animatedly, "You'll be proud of me." She wanted me to know that she'd *realized* something important: The chiropractor's sign had triggered her. The idea of removing her boots . . . that is, removing an article of clothing—*any* clothing—at anyone's insistence did, in fact, bring back feelings of exploitation from her past. Now in university, *finally* less symptomatic, she had no interest in "undressing for just anyone."

It's important in trauma therapy, to recognize our clients' triggers, but it's even more important to help them do so for themselves. They can learn to notice their triggers and to take them seriously.

In fact, for people with trauma histories, *noticing* that they'd been triggered—or are currently *being* triggered—by their environment gives them an understanding of their internal experience, their state of mind. Rather than simply feeling overwhelmed, without a sense of why, they notice *familiar feelings* . . . feelings that come up when this or that experience surfaces from their history.

Having language to contextualize experience, they find personal agency. *I was triggered by* . . . presents an empowering alternative to the self-critical stance, *I was being ridiculous*, or to some vague diffuse emotional state, *I was just totally freaked out*, without any sense of what the feelings were about, or that the feelings may have been for good reason. This is helpful, even if the client is unclear on what that reason is.

And as I mentioned, it's important for people to learn to take their triggers seriously. A question I encourage clients to ask themselves is, *What am I feeling right now . . . what might be triggering me?* Or, said another way: *What's going on for me that I'm feeling this way now?* The reflection invites people to take their internal experience seriously, to start recognizing that their states of mind shift.[3] By asking it, clients grapple with the idea that they get affected by their interpersonal world, sometimes in powerful, unpredictable ways, and that it can be unclear why.

Recognizing that they do, in fact, get triggered helps people slow down, look inside, take stock of their experience, and ask themselves what in them has bubbled to the surface. The answer doesn't need to be "correct," so to speak. The usefulness of the exercise is in the asking.

Over time, my client—the one with the winter boots—became quite good at this. Always spirited, she liked to frame the question: *What the hell was going on for me, anyway?* She asked it with self-reflectiveness, with sincerity. I liked the way she put it.

And she recognized that, when triggered, her feelings could elude her, but that they came from a real place, and had a real impact on her life.

To Firmer Ground

So triggers can be gripping. As I say above, there's a sense of being "taken back," a swift connection to traumatic experiences or to memories and emotions related to those experiences. An involuntary process, the link can be sud-

---

3. The question aims to *mentalize* their internal experience, as psychologist Peter Fonagy explains. This is discussed further in Chapter 8. See Allen et al. (2008).

den and familiar, and the person can feel overcome with a perceived sense of being unsafe. At the time, it can feel very real.

To cope in the moment, many survivors find it helpful to use *grounding* techniques. Focusing on the safety aspect of trauma treatment, psychologist Lisa Najavits (2002) described how the techniques *anchor* the person to the present and to reality.

One of the best ways to do this is to *activate sensory experiences,* to turn one's attention to the concrete, to the physical contours of one's immediate surroundings. Any of the senses can be used.

Visual activation can be valuable. This is something for therapists to keep in mind when helping clients feel grounded. Even on their own, clients can activate themselves visually. For example, psychiatrist James Chu (2011) emphasized the practical importance of light:

> One of the most basic strategies is to ensure good ambient illumination. A well-lit environment can be very helpful in grounding patients, particularly in the evening or at night. Whether in the office, hospital, or at home, this means providing adequate lighting and encouraging patients not to sit in dark or dimly lit environments when they feel anxious and vulnerable. When frightened or overwhelmed, many patients feel compelled to retreat to darkened rooms. . . . Seeking safety in such places only increases their propensity to lose their bearings in current reality and become more pulled into the flashback experience. (p. 151)

To find grounding techniques useful, clients need to be *active* participants. Focusing on familiar or comforting objects, maintaining visual contact, and naming or describing items in the immediate environment are all active ways of reengaging in the present.

One of my clients began carrying around a blank pad of paper and a pencil. When triggered, she would stop, scan her immediate surroundings, and draw. When she and I had first discussed the idea, I'd asked her to simply list the objects in her vicinity, to notice them, to name and write them down, while taking slow deep breaths. A suitable idea for some clients, it didn't entirely grab her. With pad in hand, she would draw instead. She'd slow her breathing, visually scan, and draw. *That* was something she could engage with. In this way, she took an active role in finding her *own* way of connecting to the here and now.

Any active, sensory experience can be used to help people feel grounded. Listening to music or reading out loud engages auditory sensations. Soothing odors are also grounding for some and can redirect attention. Wearing perfume on her wrists was a preferred method for one client of mine. She'd find the scent calming (although *others* weren't so pleased, so she transitioned to carrying potpourri instead).

Active physical techniques are also beneficial. Running cool water over the hands or face, feeling the ground underfoot, feeling the contours of the chair, clenching and releasing fists . . . these are all commonly used.

One fellow I treated liked to stretch and go for long walks. As a means of feeling alive and connected to the present, he would move briskly, and for a while, this worked well. But at some point, he began having difficulties with the strategy. When walking for long enough, he'd start feeling angry. He'd get triggered by others walking toward him, imagining they were threatening him, imagining the schoolteacher who had sexually assaulted him when he was a preteen. He reported one session that, recently, he'd had the urge to strike someone walking toward him.

At my suggestion, he agreed to switch strategies. The walks would be much shorter, giving just enough time for him to feel connected to the ground, but not enough for the strategy to morph into something entirely different.

That helped. And later, his walks would be to the yoga studio just down the street. There—*thankfully*—he'd never had the urge to strike anyone.

CHAPTER 6

How *Not* to Face Trauma: Strained Apologies and the Rush to Forgive

The Case of Victor

When I was a graduate student in the late 1980s, the psychological clinic at Michigan State University was housed in the basement of a tired, repurposed engineering building. Drafty in winter, oppressive in summer, and moldy throughout, with taupe linoleum flooring and cinder block walls, the only redeeming feature of the dungeon-like atmosphere was a surprisingly rich echo in some parts of the building—stairwells, restrooms, and so on. No matter *what* you sang, hummed, or whistled, it sounded great.

It was my client Victor on my first practicum who pointed this out to me: the building's only saving grace, its chance acoustic quality—not something I would have noticed myself. Singing a cappella or sometimes strumming guitar, Victor and his friend, another music major, would station themselves in one of the more resonant stairwells. Together, they would sing, often to no one in particular.

And occasionally, during the year or so that I worked with him in psychotherapy, he'd bring in cassette tapes he recorded in one of his makeshift sound studios. He was Chinese American, with a striking look—tall, broad shouldered, with a trendy mullet—this was the late 1980s, after all. Clear on his ambitions, he had a lovely singing voice and was, in fact, excelling in his music program. School wasn't the problem.

He'd originally referred himself for therapy soon after a Thanksgiving weekend. Having returned for the holiday to his home in Michigan's Upper Peninsula, he'd had a blowout argument with his younger brother, unusual in their family. They were furious with each other, and this troubled Victor.

As teenagers, about seven years earlier, Victor and Martin had sung in a successful boys' choir. Their parents were supportive, viewing their children as fortunate for the opportunity. With the choir, the brothers had toured together for two seasons—mostly in the Midwest—and even recorded a Christmas album.

In one of the last out-of-town performances of his brief choir career, Victor woke up one morning in his hotel room, groggy, in pain, lacking memory for the previous evening's events. Although he never did recall everything, later that day he told his mother all he could, when she picked up the brothers at the church parking lot. Victor was reeling, anxious, nothing like his usual contented self, worried about what had happened to him. His mother responded well, rightly insisting that he undergo a medical exam. This led to an investigation, a trial, and three years after the incident, a conviction. The truth was now known: The choirmaster, Scott, had drugged and raped Victor.

Throughout the investigation and trial, Victor's mother supported him. But their community was torn apart. There were families who stuck by them unflinchingly, and there were those who doubted the story from the start. There were many attempts at bullying. And the boys' choir, the inspired program that had brought recognition to their small, ordinary community . . . it was now dead.

On Thanksgiving weekend, just before Victor referred himself for therapy, he opened a letter that had arrived for him, just days earlier, at his family home. Although they'd recently moved, their new house was just a couple of towns over. They weren't so hard to track down.

Sharing the contents with his brother Martin, and then with his parents, Victor felt sick about the letter. And he hated how young it made him feel once again. The letter would dominate Thanksgiving, the festive dinner left virtually uneaten.

The boys had come home for the weekend from university, they'd always been close. But now they argued feverishly about the right thing to do, how to respond. After all, Martin's life had *also* been turned upside down by the rape. He wanted the past put to rest already. He, too, had lost the choir and most of his friends. He thought the answer was obvious, and their father agreed. But Victor and his mother were less certain.

The letter was a request. It came from an undisclosed address, a handwritten note from the choirmaster. It was signed simply, *Scott*.

It appealed to Victor's humanity. Straightforward, brief, the letter didn't ask for much, just one small thing: Victor's forgiveness.

To Err Is Human: The Rush to Forgive

Forgiveness has become a hot topic in popular mental health writing. Love gurus, spiritual healers, and myriad specialists all call us to its high road.

Invoking religious metaphor, pairing forgiveness with the promise of psychological health, stories abound of spontaneous generosity from those victimized most. The faster they forgive, the braver they're considered. Facing the perpetrator after so much time, having been nothing but wronged, having suffered at their hands, they feel—contrary to expectations—nothing but love.

It's a nice idea, yes. The problem with it? It's pure fiction.

In Chapter 2, I talk about how self-deception happens a lot in trauma, and that we see this in psychotherapy when clients minimize the impact of traumatic events, when they rationalize away painful experiences as having made them all the stronger, when they sidestep the emotional content of their own traumatic history. We also see self-deception when survival in the home requires ignoring reality to make everything feel more bearable, or when people recall their own stories in detached clinical terms or using mental health jargon, whitewashing the vulnerability of their true emotions.

In that chapter I also talk about the work of psychologist Peter Fonagy and colleagues (Allen et al., 2008). They have examined how those struggling in relationships represent their own and others' intentions. Drawing on philosopher Harry Frankfurt's (2005) work, Fonagy noticed that many clients function in *pretend mode*. Different from lying, which is about a deliberate misrepresentation of reality, pretend mode has more to do with misrepresenting intention. Distorting our intentions helps us fool ourselves. It makes for an *as if* quality to interactions with others.

My disagreement here is not with forgiveness per se. With true forgiveness comes great relief. Following the expression of genuine remorse, when the perpetrator takes personal responsibility, when there is atonement and restitution, forgiveness can be healing.

No, my criticism is *not* of forgiveness as such. Rather, it's with the *expectation* to forgive, it's with forced or *rushed* forgiveness. It's with the idealized, high-minded notion that there's something superior—beautiful, in fact—about survivors who can set aside their own suffering and see the world through the eyes of the perpetrator.

A motif in numerous films, books, and documentaries, it sets an expectation that, for most, lies well out of reach: *If you were the right kind of victim, a good one, you'd forgive. And if you don't, what's* wrong *with you?*

The pressure to capture this ideal makes for a rush to forgive, an *as if* forgiveness. As if, by dint of magic wand, the survivor can wave away hurt, loss, betrayal. As if forgiveness weren't a two-way street, requiring at least as much from perpetrator as from victim—*to err is human; to forgive, divine.* As if the *right* kind of survivor would aspire to the divinity forgiveness asks.

There is a culturally embedded expectation to forgive, and it comes at a heavy price: a sense of personal failing among those still haunted by their past. *Why can't I forgive already? I'm the problem.* And the rush to forgive makes for self-deception. For many, it's all too easy to emotionally disengage and pretend to themselves, to "forgive and forget."

And of course, within family and friendship circles, the expectation to forgive is strong as well. This is especially true in cases of intrafamilial trauma, when perpetrators are well known to—or even intimate with—victims. The pressure to protect the relationship, to guard secrets, to stay loyal to those we are close to . . . all make for an overwhelming pressure: *It's okay, I forgive everything.*

As if history can be swept away like that, by fiat. To the therapist, the sentiment can come across as hard-to-believe, inauthentic.

Victor wrestled with his feelings about the letter: Didn't he have an *obligation* to forgive? As a teenager, while the investigation and trial were going on, he'd received some limited counseling. And his mother, a supervising social worker with a local children's aid organization, knew what to look for; she paid close attention and spoke a lot with Victor. Despite the heaviness of their late-night talks, he would look forward to them. And largely, they were what carried him through a nasty trial. But as a high school student, he wanted to be nothing more than normal. The whole fiasco seemed well out of his hands. At the time, he would spend his counseling sessions on anything *but* the rape.

And now, early in his work with me, what Victor thought he'd long put to rest returned with a force. His feelings toward choirmaster Scott had always been mixed. He *wanted* to hate him, as supportive friends did, but to Victor it wasn't so simple. He would question himself constantly: *Wasn't the defense attorney right?* Didn't he set himself up . . . the two of them alone, watching a romantic comedy in Scott's hotel room? It wasn't like anyone had *made* him accept a drink, and then another . . .

His mother worried about Victor's self-blame. She told him all the right things: *It wasn't your fault, who gives tequila to a fifteen-year-old? Plus, he drugged you, Victor. He knew what he was doing!* Victor wasn't so sure. The experience had changed him, haunted his family, nearly destroyed his parents' marriage. That much he knew.

But so much remained unsettled. He had no clue *how* to make sense of all he'd lost, his fear of what the past said about him, his worry about what the future held in store, how to understand his and his family's history.

And here . . . here was this *letter*. He was entirely unprepared for it. I asked him, and he agreed: The letter felt much like an ambush. He was angry at Scott for sending it, yes. Still, he was ashamed. His brother forgave, his father forgave, why couldn't he? What was *wrong* with him? It all could have been far worse, after all.

That same Thanksgiving weekend, after their explosive argument, Victor's brother, frustrated, went for a long walk. And his father sat down and shared a story. It was one he'd heard on the radio, a personal heartfelt account, recollected by a jazz guitarist he'd always admired; a tale of hurt, a story of apology and how we look inside to find forgiveness. His father expressed confidence that Victor would discover a way to answer the choirmaster's apology: *But I don't want to tell you what to do . . .*

Aside from the obvious manipulation here—not lost on Victor's mother—this was the first time *apology* came up in our early discussions. That's how his father had referred to it: an apology. Up to now, Victor had called it a letter. Now, it was an apology.

I asked him, which *was* it? Was it just a letter, or was it, in fact, an apology? And how would it make a difference?

At that early point in our work, Victor didn't know. But to him, he added, it sure didn't *feel* much like an apology.

All Apologies Are *Not* Created Equal

Showing Remorse

What does a sound apology look like, one that hits the mark?

Viewing apology as a kind of remedial gesture, sociologist Erving Goffman described this social practice as having several parts: "Expression of embarrassment and chagrin; clarification that one knows what conduct had been expected and sympathizes with the application of negative sanction . . . espousal of the right way, and an avowal henceforth to pursue that course; performance of penance and the volunteering of restitution" (1971, p. 113).

It's in this tradition that, more recently, law and society scholar Richard Weisman (2014) emphasized the *showing of remorse* as central to the apology. What I like about the idea of remorse—when its expression is authentic—is that it captures a lot of what goes into a good apology.

The *emotional* nature of remorse is key. In Weisman's view, the feelings are painful, unwanted. They come spontaneously; they're not planned or deliberate. And remorse is communicated through emotional displays and gestures rather than words alone. Expressions of remorse demonstrate pain by making suffering visible.

In this sense, showing remorse is highly interpersonal. This is seen all the time in legal practice. Jurors respond poorly to defendants who don't effectively communicate remorse. Weisman wrote of the 1995 Oklahoma City bombing, "Timothy McVeigh's choice to remain mute at his execution—or 'stone-faced,' as several reporters described him—was read by most observers not as an abstention from the demand to show remorse, but as a clear expression of a lack of remorse" (2014, p. 11).

One couple I worked with came for counseling following an affair the husband had had with one of his associates. Despite all that had happened, both husband and wife said they wanted to work things out between them.

As I often do with couples, I held individual meetings with each, to better understand their early personal histories, but I don't form any "illicit pacts"—keeping secrets with one member of the couple, from the other—and I told them so.

In his individual session, the husband confessed the affair had lasted years longer than he'd admitted to before. He had a large dental practice, and he'd pretended over the years to go on many conferences with his associate, but was actually spending days away with her. The secrecy of the affair and his dishonesty were feeling unbearable to him. I encouraged him to come clean. If he wanted to do couples work, his wife would have to know the truth. So he told her, later that day.

In the next session—a meeting with the two of them—the wife was still in disbelief from the news: "You see? I can't believe a *word* that passes through his lips!" Turning to him, she said: "Aren't you sorry at all?!"

He took a deep breath, leaned forward, and looking her squarely in the eyes, replied, "I'm sorry you were lied to."

To which she marched right out, and slammed the door behind her. To his utter shock, the apology had failed.

The following week, I was astonished to see them back in my office (I'd figured they were gone forever). And we unpacked *"I'm sorry you were lied to,"* an apology so limp as to render itself lifeless. I wondered out loud about his use of the passive voice: *you were lied to.* Using language that cut off personal connection to his own actions, he was being evasive—shirking personal responsibility, keeping feelings of remorse far away.

It was an effortless, painless, self-protective apology. In his inability to show vulnerability—for remorse requires great vulnerability—he was only digging himself deeper.

This emphasis on remorse, feeling it and communicating it to survivors, is seen in the work of South African psychologist Pumla Gobodo-Madikizela (2004), who served on her country's Truth and Reconciliation Commission. She believes remorse lies at the heart of the apology: being in pain with your victim. Having recorded over forty hours of interviews with apartheid-era police colonel Eugene de Kock—who had tortured and murdered numerous anti-apartheid activists—she concluded his apology was genuine, because he expressed remorse. In an interview, Gobodo-Madikizela said: "I consider remorse to be a kind of pain. And remorse is only possible when one faces the guilt, right? And so it is a kind of reciprocal, mutual expression of a connecting with the other. . . . Remorse is feeling for the other person, and in my view, this is very important if we are engaging in conversation about the phenomenology of apology" (Kelley & Bloch, 2015).

Of course, even when a seemingly remorseful apology is expressed, not everyone is convinced. How seriously should we take it—is the apology sincere? It can be hard to gauge. Weisman (2014) reported that so-called awkward self-presentations, nonverbal signs of distress—tears, broken speech—in the National Jury Project were seen as more credible signs of remorse.

But good actors can put on a good show. And for victims, it can be hard to evaluate the genuineness of a remorseful-sounding apology.

Certainly, the original transgression offers no help in figuring this out. In the case of interpersonal trauma, we make assumptions about the internal experience of perpetrators. And these assumptions run the gamut, with some clinicians documenting that perpetrators feel "shame about being an abusive parent" (Kaufman, 1992, p. 182), and others claiming just the opposite, that true contrition in a perpetrator is a miracle of sorts (Herman, 1992).

My own research points to something in between. In one of my dissertation studies (Muller, 1993), my supervisor, John Hunter, and I looked at a large sample of both nonclinical and clinically referred fathers and mothers. These were parents whose children had already disclosed a history of violence in the home. We asked the parents to reflect on their own parenting behaviors, particularly around discipline, and we oriented them to the question of remorse: Did they feel remorseful or ashamed of themselves? Did they consider their actions wrong, and did they wish they'd had a second chance to do things differently?

What we found were broad differences; parents varied widely. Some felt remorse, and some didn't (Muller, 1993). This was true even when they reflected on their use of *severe* violence. Many considered their violent parenting behaviors as justified and appropriate, while others felt a sense of personal failure and deficiency. Perhaps not surprising, those with authoritarian belief systems and those whose spouses were also violent justified their own violent parenting practices the most (Muller, 1993, 1995, 2001a, 2001b; Muller & Hunter, 1995).

More recent studies have described similar results: In reflecting on their own behaviors, perpetrators respond with varying sentiments (Hundt & Holohan, 2012), with studies of violent women reporting more remorse than found in studies of violent men (Gaarder & Belknap, 2002; Presser, 2003). And from time to time, when I've worked clinically with perpetrators, coaching them through the process of apology and reconciliation, I've also seen broad differences in expressions of remorse. Some come across as frankly defensive; others show a kind of "canned" empathy—intellectualized, distant, performative; and still others express shame and self-reproach.

Taking Personal Responsibility

Important as it is, remorse is not the only piece of a sound apology. Criminologist Lois Presser (2003) said that in apologizing people must *take responsibility* for their actions, confirming that they did, in fact, do the deed. This kind of validation is important. The perpetrator acknowledges the victim as a person of worth, who shouldn't have been treated that way. This helps with recovery.

Let's look at the story of a veteran of the U.S. Marines, Lu Lobello, who has spoken openly about his experiences in Iraq. For a long time, Lobello wrestled with the consequences of actions he'd taken years earlier. He struggled with the question of apology, forgiveness, and how, exactly, to take responsibility. Years after a firefight in which his participation led, in part, to the death of three civilians, Lobello sought out the surviving family members whom he'd forever harmed.

In April of 2003, Lobello was a lance corporal with Fox Company, Second Battalion. It was during the start of the American-led invasion of Iraq. He was in Baghdad the day before Saddam Hussein's statue fell and was patrolling a neighborhood on foot with his squad.

It was on that day that he and his company killed three members of a local Iraqi family, the Kachadoorians. Confused and frightened, the family had been trying to make their way home when, mistakenly, they found themselves in the middle of a nighttime firefight, at a major five-way intersection.

The marines opened fire on the family's vehicles, not realizing they were shooting at civilians. In an interview, Lobello described what happened next: "After shooting, that's when the mother started waving a white t-shirt, which was pretty much stained red from the blood in the car, and started screaming, 'We're peace people.' They were screaming, 'We're Christians, we're Christians, we're peace people. Why'd you shoot my husband, why'd you shoot my father, why'd you shoot my son, why'd you shoot my brother?'" (Kelley & Bloch, 2015).

Years after discharge, feeling alienated from his military life, struggling with symptoms of posttraumatic stress disorder and substance abuse, Lobello painstakingly sought out and found the surviving members of the Kachadoorian family, who had, to his great surprise, moved to California. His attempts to reach them led, eventually, to a rather tense face-to-face meeting. Reflecting on his wish to do right by the Kachadoorian family, and on taking responsibility, Lobello said:

> No matter if you're taking responsibility, or if you're saying you're sorry, just the act of owning up to your role, whatever that may be, in a tragic situation, I think is the real message, and the real power to be had. The whole act of being in war leads to a lot of questions of morality, of sinning, of being a saint, what's right, what's wrong. So if you have a day that you kill a bad guy, and then you accidentally kill a civilian because they're caught in the line of fire, well, you're a sinner *and* a saint. And you have to reconcile these things now for the rest of your life. (Kelley & Bloch, 2015)

When we speak of taking responsibility, we mean *personal* responsibility. The late comedian Flip Wilson's oft-repeated line, *The devil made me do it*, comes to mind. Playing a character whose modus operandi was to shirk responsibility at every turn, what made the line so funny was how earnest Wilson was in the delivery, as if *anyone* were to blame but him.

In interpersonal trauma, people make choices—often choices representing great personal harm to another. An apology can't be authentic without a *personal* reckoning. Without it, what we have is a botched apology, one that misses the mark. Rather than helping, it actually makes the survivor feel worse. It's an apology that makes for missed opportunity.

Recall the couple I'd worked with where the dentist-husband had had an affair, and how, in one of the sessions, he tried to apologize as best as he could: *I'm sorry you were lied to.*

What about this apology made his wife so angry? As I describe above, in the next session I pointed out his use of passive voice. That resonated for her. She said she hadn't been able to put her finger on it, but yeah, that really upset her. In fact, up to that point, he'd never actually *claimed* the act of lying, not really—not where he was personally holding himself to account.

Using language that cut off all personal responsibility, it was as though, throughout the affair, he was simply along for the ride. The restaurants, the hotels, the weekends away with his associate-girlfriend, covert telephone calls to her during family vacations . . . as if he'd taken no part in those choices.

His use of passive voice had made the apology insincere, thoroughly *im*personal. And in doing so, what appeared now was a botched apology. Gobodo-Madikizela said: "Usually what we find is that perpetrators stop at the point of guilt. They will acknowledge some, but mostly deny. People justifying, because we saw this at the truth commission as well, perpetrators came and they said, 'I did it, but it was a war. I did it, but I was obeying orders'" (Kelley & Bloch, 2015).

What's Wrong With the Rush to Forgive?

Rushed Forgiveness Makes for Self-Deception

As I said earlier, my intent here isn't to beat up on forgiveness. In the context of authentic remorse, when the perpetrator takes personal responsibility for past choices, when there's movement toward restitution, forgiveness can bring great relief.

But *rushed* forgiveness is different altogether. It comes, in part, from culturally embedded expectations. When victims are depicted as setting aside their own suffering, when they rise above, so to speak, reaching within their hearts to forgive, this is characterized among popular spiritual leaders, writers, and journalists—almost to the point of cliché—as both moving and profound.

It's an ideal that turns personal responsibility on its head. Why can't we all just "move on" already? *It's that stubborn victim's fault.* There are numerous examples of survivors who've endured years of secret abuse from widely beloved community members, and they finally speak out—only to find disbelief and public scorn.

And as I said earlier, the ideal is unreachable for most. It leads to a sense of personal failure. *Everyone else has moved on. What's wrong with me?* The expectation to forgive can become a burden, a pressure to conjure feelings that aren't there, or to cover up those that are.

For people who've internalized this expectation—*forgiveness is right, noble—*

the rush toward it makes for self-deception. This is a problem because it undermines trauma work. The temptation to cut off painful feelings, to sweep away loss and suffering, as if all were forgiven, forgotten . . . for many, this represents a powerful draw, a wish to "get over it" already. But trauma work takes time. It's hard to face an overwhelming past.

The attempt to short-cut the process by rushing forgiveness is to be dishonest with ourselves. It becomes a tool of avoidance, *pretending* the pain is all gone. It sidesteps hurt and anger, it circumvents mourning . . . squelching, rather than facing our personal histories.

And sometimes therapists, too, can be deceived by rushed forgiveness. I've seen this with supervisees. In *Trauma and the Avoidant Client* (2010), I wrote: "For the therapist, it is tempting to hear the language of forgiveness and to regard the individual with admiration, to see him as mature, strong, impressive. I have sometimes heard students presenting such cases, referring to the client as having a 'remarkable attitude'" (p. 83).

Stories of overcoming pain and adversity . . . we all like stories like these. When we hear people use the language of forgiveness, this can be very compelling, even gratifying. It puts a positive ending on an otherwise tragic story. It can bring great satisfaction to the listener.

And when clients speak the language of forgiveness with therapists who ideologically *value* it, this can also pose a problem. Is the client, in some subtle way, performing? Doing as they imagine a good survivor should? If so, therapist and client, together, may be operating in pretend mode, colluding to "wrap up" a traumatic story rather than face it sincerely.

For therapists, when they hear the language of forgiveness, especially early in therapy, it's important to *notice ambivalence*. On the face of it, the client may be responding to internal and external pressures, rushing into forgiveness, using the language before they've really worked through painful feelings about the trauma. But when we notice ambivalence, we *listen* for mixed feelings about the trauma. These aren't always evident; they may come out in subtler ways, as I point out in previous chapters.

Psychotherapy is about helping us appreciate our own complexities, finding lost parts of ourselves. Like many of our important emotional experiences, forgiveness is a *process*. It changes as we do. It's active, not passive or static. We look at this next.

The Rush Toward Forgiveness Undermines
the *Process* of Forgiveness

How we think about our traumatic experiences can change as we do. As we confront different life challenges or milestones—finding or losing love, parenting—as we struggle with loss, with medical illness, or with the aging of loved ones . . . as we grow and develop, past experiences can feel very different over time, sometimes better, sometimes worse. That is, as new life events unfold, new feelings about the past unfold as well.

But the statement, *It's okay, I forgive everything*—this is a lot to commit to. I don't recommend saying the words lightly. It frames the past as having been left behind. It impresses a certain expectation on the survivor. And if it's a statement arrived at hastily, it unnecessarily boxes the person in. The rush to forgive is emotionally limiting.

Why is this a problem? Because it imposes a certain definitiveness, a finality, a closure that doesn't match the way we actually go through life. We see this with our clients. For example, the fellow who becomes a new father—this experience may recast the way he views his own parents' contentious divorce. Or the young professor triggered by the suicide of a colleague, long having put her own mother's suicide to rest. Feelings of hurt, disappointment, as well as empathy and understanding, can all emerge anew. People can feel differently about the same past events, at different points in their lives. And the rush to forgive closes the door. It wraps everything up so neatly.

But people aren't neat—they're rather messy. Personal feelings about traumatic events can vary when we're in different states of mind, and as we grow, develop, and change. Forgiveness doesn't *have* to be declared quickly, or definitively. It can be partial, or not at all, or a process that shifts about, or one that comes together over time.

For therapists, it's important to give clients permission to view forgiveness as something that may come and go, one that has its ups and downs. It's useful to *notice aloud* the client's emerging wish to forgive (or a newfound reluctance to), paying attention to how and when this may have *shifted* over the course of their lifespan.

Perhaps the client finds a reemergence of memories or feelings from long ago—they're once again angry at the perpetrator, and even at themselves for "this crap from the past," as they put it. After all, they'd long ago "forgiven," so really, they *shouldn't* be angry anymore. And yet, here they are, once again losing sleep, preoccupied by the trauma, full of feeling. With curiosity, we notice this aloud. In their life story, *what's shifting for them*? When they previously "forgave," where were they at? And what's changed? *What may be going on for them now*, now that overwhelming feelings—long thought to be gone—have returned?

Or with the client who finds themselves, for the first time in a long while, surprisingly open to a family relationship they'd written off ages ago, due to, say, early abuse. Why now? How can we better understand this emotional shift in them?

In this way, we view forgiveness as a psychological *process*—we give it shape, color. Over the course of our lives, forgiveness can take twists and turns. In therapy, this is far more helpful than seeing it as static—or framing it as a virtue.

The Rush to Forgive Is Morally Compromising

When trauma survivors make the decision to forgive, they may not realize it but they adopt a particular moral position. Of course, sometimes that can be fine. But when people grant forgiveness hastily—in the rush to tuck away the past—they may be declaring something inadvertently, something they don't truly believe. Along the way, they're compromising themselves, undermining their own sense of justice, undercutting their own dignity and self-respect.

Philosopher Maria Magoula Adamos (2011), a scholar in the study of mind and emotion, asks us to consider when forgiveness might not be such a good thing. She says that forgiveness can be used as an impediment to justice, or even as a license for continuing *injustice*.

Putting the issue into historical perspective, Adamos goes to the works of Aristotle, who in the *Nicomachean Ethics* emphasized the importance and usefulness of anger—when circumstances call for it—saying that sometimes anger is not only justified but also required. Adamos thinks that, by taking our anger seriously, especially in the context of an injustice, we are taking justice itself seriously and, in fact, taking *ourselves* seriously.

In a poignant historical example of rushed forgiveness and how it can compromise justice and our own values, Adamos points to the writing of *Slate* senior editor Dahlia Lithwick. In her sobering 2009 piece "Forgive Not," Lithwick describes the Obama administration's reluctance to investigate and prosecute senior Bush-era officials who authorized torture and warrantless surveillance. Lithwick wrote that, in the United States, there was a national appetite to "move on."

Lithwick sharply warns of the consequences when we rush to forgive, implying how easy a return to torture would be. Lamenting the cavalier dismissal of past atrocities, she wrote: "We are telling ourselves that bad people did bad things under bad circumstances, but that it's better to forgive and forget, that we are really truly sorry and it won't happen again. We are like a nation of drunks after a bender. We are full of good intentions, but unwilling to hold ourselves to account" (2009).

For our purposes, why does this matter? Because when we forgive, we make a statement, to others and to ourselves: *I forgive you.* It's a big statement. It implies acceptance, understanding, closure. It suggests finality. Again, all this is fine in principle, but when that forgiveness was rushed, when it came from some kind of self-imposed duress, there's a price to be paid.

When people compromise their own sense of justice, they compromise *themselves.* They undermine their dignity and devalue their self-respect. And they're left with a disturbing sense of self-betrayal.

This happens a lot in trauma, especially early in the treatment. As people struggle to make sense of their painful history, wanting desperately to "get past it," they tell themselves and others that they forgive, putting misgivings or mixed feelings out of mind. In the process, they betray an important part of themselves, the part that seeks justice. They betray their own dignity.

Let's revisit the case of Victor from earlier in this chapter. Of the many things Victor and I discussed, it was this sense of *injustice* that resonated with him the most, it irritated and motivated him.

Recall how Victor had been drugged and raped by his choirmaster, Scott. The investigation, the trial, the conviction—it all caused untold stress on the family and divided the community. And recall how Victor and his brother Martin were thrown into turmoil over the issue of forgiveness, when Scott's letter arrived requesting just that. Even their parents were divided in their opinions. Dad was much more inclined than Mom to grant the request—he *wanted* his son to forgive.

Victor struggled with his feelings about the letter, partly regarding it his obligation to forgive, worried he'd disappoint his father if he didn't. He blamed himself for being in Scott's hotel room at all. He wrestled with questions of his own sexuality. *Doesn't this all prove I'm gay?* He did have a girlfriend—a cellist in the music program—still, it turned out, his sexuality wasn't all that clear to him just yet, and this made him anxious.

Part of the work was developmental, helping him sit with the idea of *not knowing*. His sexual orientation might get clearer with time and experience, but he couldn't *make* himself know just yet. And part of the work centered on how hard he'd been on himself, how he'd justified the rape as punishment for his sexual feelings—as if his *attraction* to a man somehow excused being *raped* by a man.

The theme of injustice resonated for Victor. How unfair it was: the friends that he and his family had lost, the years spent consumed by legal fallout, the fact that they'd eventually had to leave the community, and, ultimately, how unfair that the rape had happened at all.

But also, Victor came to understand the injustice he'd inflicted on *himself*: how he'd blamed himself not only for the rape, but also for the suffering his family had gone through afterward; for the bullying his brother would endure until he changed schools, for the anxious late-night conversations he'd overhear his parents having throughout the trial.

And, during the year or so that Victor and I worked together, the issue of forgiveness would come up less and less, mostly, it seemed, because he *felt* it less.

He didn't rule out forgiveness altogether. Perhaps . . . at some point. But for now, it just didn't feel honest. His father's understanding was important to him, so on a visit home, Victor told him: "Not yet."

Maybe someday . . . he didn't know. But he wasn't prepared to forgive yet. And maybe he never would.

He hoped his father would understand. But even if the choice was wrong, it was, at least, his to make.

CHAPTER 7

Mourning the Losses That Trauma Brings

Many spiritual paths begin with the awareness of suffering. The Buddha leaves his comfortable life when he first encounters old age, sickness, and death outside the palace walls. The Children of Israel come of age only after centuries of slavery—and with ancestors said to have wandered, struggled, and mourned. Christ in the wilderness and on the cross, Arjuna on the battlefield. And although spirituality today is alleged by its critics to be narcissistic and escapist, anyone who takes contemplative practice seriously finds instead an uncovering of that which was hidden—and as a consequence, a confrontation with pain.

—Rabbi Jay Michaelson, *The Gate of Tears*

The Case of Angelina

When I began working with Angelina, I'd never received formal training in the area of substance abuse. But having recently finished my clinical fellowship, now with a budding private practice, I was hungry for referrals. A year into owning our first home, my wife and I had a toddler in diapers and twins on the way. Money was tight, referrals were scarce. And it wasn't like Boston was hard up for psychodynamic therapists—it never was.

Maybe I was hitting a patch of luck, because that week, it seemed, everyone other than me had decided to go on summer vacation. My friend—who was calling to refer a client—implied as much when we spoke by phone, enumerating the *sheer number* of therapists he'd tried to reach before me. Not a great feeling—just how low *was* I on his list, anyway? Still, a referral was a referral; I wasn't going to be picky.

And although my friend knew I had a fledgling practice in trauma therapy, *his* work was mostly in substance abuse. That was how he met Angelina to begin with. He'd seen her for some crisis work, first in the emergency department, and then in the outpatient psychiatry clinic of one of the Longwood hospitals. Her boyfriend had brought her in a few weeks prior. She'd made a suicide attempt earlier that evening, having swallowed a couple dozen Tylenol, along with a bottle of wine.

Fed up with her drinking, and all that went with it, her boyfriend broke up with her then and there, in the waiting area, apparently making quite a show of it.

Although problem drinking, admittedly, wasn't my main focus, I took the case and began working with her in outpatient therapy. At the time (the mid-1990s), few therapists were working from what is now called a trauma-informed perspective. Psychologist Catherine Classen and colleagues explained that when therapists work from this framework, they incorporate an understanding of how violence and psychological trauma affect peoples' lives. They're aware that traumatic events aren't rare, but are common in their communities (Clark, Classen, Fourt, & Shetty, 2015).[1]

I wondered—even in our first meeting—if Angelina had experienced an early trauma history. An executive assistant, Angelina spent most of the session complaining about her on-off boyfriend, Gary, who was also her boss; he was the head of a large pet food company. I couldn't quite tell *how* she viewed him. Was it with admiration, mistrust, contempt? They certainly had an immature relationship. While still in crisis intervention, days after he'd broken up with her, he showed up with tickets to Las Vegas. They had makeup sex early that evening, and presto, they were together again.

I asked her for a story about their relationship. She explained that, following the suicide attempt, she took a week off work. After that, she added, she was "all better." Her first morning back, Gary told her she'd be attending a meeting. Several of the vice-presidents would be there. As his executive assistant, she'd have to take careful notes. The company was introducing a new line, and this was important. She was instructed to bring several cans of the new product, and she complied nervously, suspecting something was up.

She didn't want to watch, but couldn't help herself, as her boyfriend

---

1. A good description of *trauma-informed care* can be found in Clark et al. (2015).

directed each vice-president in turn to try, and to comment on, the cat food plated in front of them. Apparently, he took it all quite seriously. Was it a test of their allegiance, a cruel joke, a show of command? There was a certain sadistic elegance to the exercise: the cat food had been served on fine china. And a quasi-scientific tone had been adopted as well, like some bizarre focus group. Angelina had to carefully record each vice-president's comments. Of course, they described how *delicious* the new product was, as if they had any other choice.

I asked Angelina, as she recounted the story, what was going on for her—what was she feeling? *Sick inside*, she said. She could only watch as, one by one, they were humiliated by her boyfriend. The whole to-do made her feel weak and pathetic—she couldn't, or wouldn't, do anything to intervene. She didn't even want to think about it—she tried not to. It upset her too much.

And yet, after all she'd just shared, she was still *with* him. How did she understand that? To which she responded, as if the answer were entirely self-evident: Because she loved him, and he *needed* her.

Angelina's early trauma history became clearer when we did an attachment interview, the next session. Recall from Chapter 1 how the Adult Attachment Interview (AAI) invites clients to think about their early experiences with caregivers and helps determine their understanding of attachment—how they think about the world of relationships (George et al., 1996; Hesse, 1999; Steele & Steele, 2008). Almost halfway through the interview, the person is typically asked to reflect on whether they were ever *frightened or worried as a child*. Angelina responded with:

Uhm . . . worried? I don't know . . . There was this one time I remember, where my parents almost broke up for good. And, I'm not sure if this is right, but this is how I remember it. They were just fighting and fighting, sometimes it would get really crazy. My dad would drink a lot after work, and my mom would get in his face . . . and he was a lot bigger than her, and he'd throw her around and hit her. But this one time, they just kept yelling. And they said okay, that's it, we're getting divorced. I think I was twelve then. And my twin sister started freaking out. I told her to try to do homework, or to listen to music, not to pay attention to what was going on. But she was just crying and crying, she didn't know what to do with herself. And I—mature little girl that I am—went upstairs, stood between my parents, and started asking them questions. I'm like, okay, so what happened? . . . and yada yada yada. And, I mediated the situation, and I dealt with it. And I didn't really get any answers from them, so much as I calmed everyone down. And I asked like, okay, so why are you fighting now? . . . and yada yada yada. Just questions like that. What a twelve-year-old thinks their parents need. And I said, can't we find a solution? . . . can't we find a compromise? So, they didn't answer any of the questions, they just listened to my questions. They calmed down, everybody calmed down. They told me to go to bed. They sent my sister to bed. They spoke about it, dealt with it, and they stayed together.

(pause) So . . . I credit myself. That might have been a time where I was worried, but no, I didn't worry or anything, as a child.

Let's unpack this a bit. Here we see some familiar themes. One that comes across loud and clear is that of *self-deception*. As I've said, self-deception often accompanies trauma. It's a way of managing emotional pain. We see this when clients minimize the impact of traumatic events, when they put a positive spin, or a positive ending on dreadful personal stories, when they rationalize away overwhelming experiences: *That's what all parents did back then.* Or, *It's good that it happened, I'm a better person for it.*

We also see self-deception when feelings are turned off. Emotions are cut out of the narrative, protecting the client from what is otherwise intolerable. Psychiatrist James Chu explained that "a person who is experiencing avoidant symptoms can have cognitive awareness of the trauma, but the affect and meaning of the experience can be split off (e.g., 'I can remember what happened, but I feel numb and I'm confused about how to think about it')" (2011, p. 47).

Here, Angelina wrestles with a personal question about whether she was ever *frightened or worried* as a child, a question that confronts her directly with the issue of her own vulnerability. Avoidance permeates her response.

Right from the get-go, she changes the very question from "frightened or worried" to simply "worried." The word *frightened* is just too much to take. It's an emotion that makes her feel far too vulnerable. Yet, her history is just that: *frightening*. In her own words, her parents' interactions would get really crazy. In fact, her mother would sometimes end up in the hospital, the domestic violence would get so bad. As for her twin sister—she's crying in the story, terrified her parents will finally separate. But Angelina? She flips into *pretend mode*, as if she were a daytime talk-show host (or an imagined couples therapist). This twelve-year-old marches upstairs, takes control of the situation, and manages by interviewing her parents.

But what makes this a good example of self-deception is *how* she recounts the story. It's told as a story of heroism. *She* saved her parents' marriage. *She* rescued *them*, saying, *I calmed everyone down. They stayed together. I credit myself.* And what's deleted from the story are the emotions a preteen would actually feel, a child who knows her mother might end up, yet again, in the hospital, or eventually dead.

The feelings of fear and anxiety that arise when family safety is compromised, when there's ongoing domestic conflict, when basic needs are only sporadically met—these were left out of the narrative. She concludes her recollection by emphasizing it *might* have been a time when she was worried, but no, she didn't worry or anything as a child.

And as I would find out soon enough, in this family daily life was infused with trauma and substance abuse. With virtually no formal education, speaking no English, her parents had, years earlier, emigrated to the United States from the Azores region of Portugal, where they'd had a small dairy farm. When Angelina was in grade school, her father struggled to find employment, and they began moving from town to town in New England, his problem drinking worsening each time he would lose a job. Settling in a poor Boston suburb, he found work as a driver, shuffling cars at an auto body shop, and her mother cleaned homes, earning twice her husband's salary, frustrating him to no end.

"Sob story," Angelina would say.

Every few months, Dad would come home drunk and would, in Angelina's words, "kick the crap" out of her mother. But Angelina wanted no pity party, as she put it. She didn't want to be a victim or to sit around wallowing in misery. Besides, she added, her mother "did *nothing* to stand up to him." Even as Angelina would congratulate herself for keeping her parents' marriage together, she complained her mother did nothing to end it. *She could've taken us away, she could've left him!*

And Angelina sure didn't want to blame it on growing up poor, as her twin sister did. The one close friend she had in junior high school she had to leave behind. Dad was seeking a better-paying job—they had to move yet again. This would be the first of several times when Angelina tried to kill herself. Leaving her best friend forever, she would later tell me, was the worst of it, the toughest part of all. She took pills that morning, regretting it almost immediately, vomiting it up. But later that very day she made it home from school in time to make supper for the family, one of her many home responsibilities.

She contributed to the rent with a part-time job, she cooked, she cleaned. She refused to be a bother.

She had learned to take care of others.

It's in this context that we see another important theme in her attachment interview, a pattern that psychiatrist Salvador Minuchin (1974, 2012) noticed in the *parental child*. Explained succinctly by psychologist Gregory Jurkovic (1997), when children are *parentified*, family dynamics overburden them with the responsibility of protecting and sustaining parents, siblings, and the family as a whole. Why is this a problem? In Minuchin's words: "The potential exists that parental children will become symptomatic when they are given responsibilities that they cannot handle, or are not given the authority to carry out their responsibilities. Parental children are, by definition, caught in the middle" (Minuchin & Fishman, 1981, p. 54).

And I didn't discover until we'd been working together a few months just how parentified and "caught in the middle" Angelina was. Once when she was a young teenager, her mom found Dad, late in the night, passed out in the kitchen. Inebriated, disoriented, he had hit the floor with a thump, having pulled some small appliances down with him, making quite the racket. It was *Angelina* who had to keep her wits about her. He was bleeding badly from his mouth, and Mom panicked. And throughout the night, it was Angelina who remained with her father in the emergency department, serving as Portuguese-English translator for the doctor, having sent her mother home—hours earlier—in a cab.

In Angelina's AAI response, we see this theme in full relief: Her pattern of taking care of others, of serving as the voice of reason, of being the adult in the room. As she said: "They were like, okay, that's it, we're getting divorced . . . And I—mature little girl that I am—went upstairs, stood between my parents, and started asking them questions . . . They calmed down, everybody calmed down . . . I credit myself."

Facing a Lost Childhood

How children learn to manage their psychological environment depends a lot on what is contained and tolerated in the relationship with the caregiver—so said attachment theorist Arietta Slade (2004). When people grow up with abuse or neglect in the home, when physical, emotional, and psychological needs of children are set aside, when safe spaces are few and far between, children learn to adapt.

To protect the relationship with caregivers, children accommodate to the caregiver's needs. This is especially true in traumatizing homes, where psychological resources are scarce and survival depends on towing the line.

When parents are emotionally incapacitated, distracted, unable to carry out the caregiving role, many children accommodate, coming to value others' needs above their own, parenting their own parents. And the loss they experience is profound. Childhood needs are subverted, set aside. And in time, they're lost altogether. Jurkovic wrote: "Perhaps the greatest loss experienced by destructively parentified children is loss of childhood, although the bitterness, disappointment, depression, and other effects of this deprivation may not be realized until later in their lives" (1997, p. 51).

Loss of childhood is one of the common effects of growing up in a traumatizing home. Yet, as Jurkovic points out above, its consequences aren't felt until later in adulthood, making it a loss that's hard to pin down, for many hard to notice at all. This is especially true for those who manage vulnerable emotions by cutting them off, for those who set aside rejection, hurt, and the loss inherent in trauma.

When Feelings Are Cut Off

We see a striking emotional disconnection in Angelina's case. This is someone who had, several times throughout her life tried to kill herself. Yet, with just a week off work, following her latest suicide attempt, she describes herself as "all better," as if the whole time all she'd had was the flu.

Boston psychologist, the late Leigh McCullough noticed that, at the center of many psychiatric disorders, people are afraid of their own emotional responses (McCullough & Andrews, 2001). They have internal conflicts about their own feelings. Referring to the phenomenon as "affect phobias,"[2] McCullough and Andrews (2001) wrote:

> Patients who are afraid to express anger or assert themselves may cry, feel depressed, act compliantly, or withdraw. Patients who are afraid of experiencing grief may chuckle to lighten up, become numb, or choke back tears. Patients who are too embarrassed or frightened to show tenderness or care for another may put on a "tough front" or devalue the other person. (p. 83)

As I would discover in later sessions, Angelina had *always* toughed it out. Getting upset as a kid? Seeking comfort? Crying? Not an option. Disconnecting from her pain, she had learned to cut off her feelings. But her feelings were there, and they could be destructive, almost always to herself.

Through this lens, let's look again at Angelina's AAI response. Where is the *emotion*? This is the story of a family in distress, out of control. And Angelina? She's the stoic. In her telling, Mom and Dad are "fighting and fighting," threatening to break up for good. Sister is "crying and crying," distraught, no idea what to do. To which Angelina steels herself, marches upstairs, and, like the executive assistant she'd later become, manages. She manages her parents and her twin sister—she manages everyone.

I've often presented this case to audiences of therapists, and I've asked them what they felt as they heard the clip from Angelina's AAI. Along with an awkward discomfort, a sense of disbelief, and anger at the parents, the feeling of sadness almost always comes up.

As Angelina told the story, she laughed—perhaps on some level recognizing how absurd the whole thing was. But as I heard it, I felt sad for her. I felt sad she was burdened with rescuing her family, sad she had to save her parents from themselves, sad she had no opportunity to be a child. *I* felt the sadness Angelina couldn't . . . I felt it on her behalf.

As I've mentioned throughout, recovery from trauma is, in part, finding a

---

2. A research review of McCullough's affect phobia treatment model can be found in Julien and O'Connor (2017).

way to tell our most painful life stories. It's a search for a coherent narrative, one that has personal meaning, one that doesn't utterly overwhelm or tear us apart inside.

And simply "talking about" what happened in a removed, dispassionate, clinical way isn't enough. It doesn't capture the full extent of the experience, it has little concrete value. Psychiatrist Judith Herman explained this well when she wrote: "The recitation of facts without the accompanying emotions is a sterile exercise, without therapeutic effect. As Breuer and Freud (1893–95/1955) noted a century ago, 'recollection without affect almost invariably produces no result.' At each point in the narrative, therefore, the patient must reconstruct not only what happened but also what she felt" (1992, p. 177).

Working with loss means helping the client connect to emotions that are hard to bear, feelings the person would rather, in part, leave by the wayside. For people with histories of trauma, there are so many losses.

Acknowledging those losses is frightening—it makes the client feel vulnerable. For therapists, it requires *listening for* themes of rejection, hurt, and other uncomfortable emotions that go along with loss, like sadness and pain. It also means paying close attention to the feelings that get stirred in us—emotions too frightening for the client to experience directly. With people like Angelina, these are feelings so easy to miss, as the client is motivated to sidestep them the moment they come up.

And as therapists, when we work with people who cut off their own emotions, when we find ourselves feeling what they can't, part of the undertaking is to help them discover a way to sit with their own pain,[3] to bear their overwhelming losses.

Making Emotional Connections

To face the losses that trauma brings, we must face difficult feelings. Mourning means opening up to personal vulnerabilities. As clients, it means putting ourselves in a psychological space that is, at a minimum, stirring and confusing and, more typically, upending and painful.

We face realities that question our illusions about the world, like *Childhood is*

---

3. More on helping traumatized clients connect to their emotional experiences can be found in Cordeiro, Rependa, Muller, and Foroughe (2018).

happy, carefree. We ask questions that have no simple answers: *Why was I stuck with a tyrant at home? Why did no one try to stop him?* Chu (2011) wrote:

> Full realization of the extent of their abuse, and the subsequent toll it has taken on their lives, allows patients to begin to mourn the losses that have resulted from the abuse—those things they have missed and those things that couldn't happen as a result of their victimization. This slow and painful process may involve patients examining each significant aspect of their pasts and reframing their understanding of the events and their meaning. (p. 126)

When therapists work with loss, when they help people connect to painful feelings, they help them discover aspects of *themselves*—vulnerable parts that had been cut off long ago. And in time, as remembered experiences are viewed through an emotional lens, context changes. Stories gain form and color, and meaning changes.

Let's look at an interchange between Angelina and me about halfway through her eleventh session of therapy. It's in this meeting that we see an important shift. She came in telling me about a crisis that erupted at work. She'd been given the task of firing one of the administrative staff, an excellent assistant, a friend who'd recently seen her through some tough times.

Weeks earlier, Angelina had described her sense of personal responsibility for others, even at work, at the time expressing pride she was forever the "go-to" person in the office. If any of the admin staff had a problem, professional or personal, Angelina was the one they talked to first. So this firing felt to her friend, to all the admin staff—to Angelina herself—as an affront, as a personal betrayal. Her boyfriend-boss, Gary, had insisted she do it. She protested, considering it arbitrary. But, backed into a corner, she did as she was told. And now, she didn't know who to hate more, Gary or herself.

At this point in the therapy session, the conversation shifted to how she'd always done as expected, fixed everyone else's problems—how she'd always been the "responsible" one in the room.

Angelina: (raising her voice) What's *wrong* with me?! I mean, really, there's seriously something messed up about me. Why do I have to be so god-damned compliant?! I know why . . . because I've always been very responsible and stuff. Because people have always ended up relying on me. And now, here I am again, just doing as I'm . . . just doing as I'm tol— (voice trails off incomprehensibly).

(She's silent for about five seconds, thinking.)

Muller: (tentatively) Doing as I'm . . . told?

Angelina: (nods silently) Yeah . . . doing as I'm told. (pause) Wow . . . that sounds kinda cold.

Muller: Does it sound that way to you?

Angelina: A little bit. (long pause) Yeah.

Muller: (nods) Okay. And . . . if that's true that that sounds cold (Angelina starts to bite her nails) what would that say about *you*?

Angelina: (bites nails) A little bit cold.

Muller: (nods) It would say that?

Angelina: (nods) Yeah . . . yeah (looks down and away, pensive).

Muller: Angelina . . . what are you feeling right now?

Angelina: Kinda . . . I don't know. I mean . . . I think I've always had to be cold.

Muller: (nods) How so?

Angelina: Well, I'm not totally sure . . . but, I think so. I don't know if it was because we just came here, me and my family. Basically, you immigrate from where you're at, and you come to this new place. We just sort of uprooted, you know? We have some members of the family that came before we did. But really, we were all kinda scattered. So it's just, it always felt like there was just no . . . there was no good reason to have any connection to anything. I always felt, because it's just, I don't know . . . it's not like I have any roots or ties here. My family wasn't connected to anything. Or to anyone. At least, if I would've had a close family—or if we weren't so crazy . . . I can see why people in those kinds of situations have clear ties. But with me, I just feel like (voice starts to quiver) sort of like, I had a cold makeshift community of just different people who were around (eyes redden with tears, briefly) and, you just, you make the best of who's around. But it's never gonna be the ideal situation of having a *real* family. Like, it's just not ever gonna be like that (pensive).

Muller: (nods) You're feeling a lot right now.

Angelina: Yeah . . .

Muller: What *are* you feeling?

Angelina: Uhm, (pause) well, (pause) that on the flip side, I just feel like that's the way it is but . . . I also always felt, that it would have been nice (voice starts to quiver) to have been in that place (voice quivering) where you *have* those connections, and you're settled—and you're with people who love you and want you. And you don't feel like you have to leave, or you wanna leave, or it doesn't make a difference if you leave (tears). It just would've been nice (tears) to have been in a family like that. But it's just too bad . . . and that's just—that's how I feel. (long pause) It's just kinda sad . . .

Muller: (softly) Yeah . . . yeah, you're feeling sad about that . . .

Angelina: Yeah (long pause). Yeah (wipes eyes of tears).

Let's think about this segment. It took place in the eleventh meeting of a treatment lasting about a year. Up to then, I'd rarely seen Angelina express much emotion; in fact, this was the first time I saw her cry. The session represents an important moment for her, and between us, when she, and our working relationship, shifts.

She begins to let down her guard, to look inside, and to do so in a way that feels authentic to us both. What begins as unbearable self-loathing—for having betrayed her close friend by firing her—shifts to anger, a productive anger that opens a door.

None of this *had* to happen. She could have simply clammed up during the session, gone home, and perhaps tried to kill herself. She'd certainly attempted suicide before, always around the prospect of losing close others. But instead, what takes place? She finds an angry voice, one that scolds: *What's wrong with me?! Why do I have to be so god-damned compliant?!* It's angry, yes, but it's also a voice that propels, one that confronts. Indignant, she faces the person-pleaser within—the part of her that takes care of others, at her own expense—and she now demands change, as if to say enough is enough: enough doing as expected, enough playing the martyr, enough putting up with abuse.

And with the expression of her anger—using it as a segue—she adopts an inward-looking stance, engaging in a process that's new to her, one that's a bit troubling but, as she stays with it, unburdening.

As she looks inside, recognizing what she's done to a close friend, she's fueled by distress and anger at herself—furious at the compliant part of her that does as told. But she's also alarmed, surprised to see a coldness in her own actions—

Wow . . . that sounds kinda cold. And again, rather than berating herself, the two of us explore with curiosity. My questions help simply by clearing the way.

Where does exploration of herself as "cold" take her? She progresses to: *My family wasn't connected to anything. Or to anyone.* As her voice starts to quiver, as her eyes redden with tears, I notice she's full of feeling. And as she realizes she grew up in a *cold makeshift community of just different people who were around*, I ask her what she's experiencing inside; I'm interested in what she's feeling *in the moment*.

And where does she land? At a place of yearning, where there's a longing for what might have been—where there's a loss of the *relationship* that might have been. Now vulnerable, she opens herself up to feelings of sadness and loss.

Poignantly, tearfully, she affirms an unspoken wish: *It would have been nice to have been in that place, where you have those connections, and you're settled— and you're with people who love you and want you. And you don't feel like you have to leave, or you wanna leave, or it doesn't make a difference if you leave.*

To have been in a family where she mattered, to have felt wanted—this is fundamental and, really, not asking for much. But recognizing its absence is such a painful loss.

Writer Judith Viorst considers loss universal and unavoidable, indeed a *necessary* part of life, because, in her words, we grow by losing and leaving and letting go. Viorst wrote: "Throughout our life we grow by giving up. We give up some of our deepest attachments to others. We give up certain cherished parts of ourselves. We must confront, in the dreams we dream, as well as in our intimate relationships, all that we never will have and never will be . . . And sometimes, no matter how clever we are, we must lose" (1986, p. 16).

Loss is necessary for growth and development. So too, *facing* loss is necessary to grow from trauma. It's key to telling our story honestly, key to finding a coherent narrative.

Central to Angelina's therapy, she connects to loss on a personal, emotional level. It helps her with the difficult task of putting her own experiences into perspective. Clients mourn, in James Chu's words, "those things they have missed and those things that couldn't happen as a result of their victimization" (2011, p. 126).

And for Angelina, mourning became an opportunity for exploration. Like I mention above, the eleventh session represented a pivotal moment in the treatment—there were shifts in her, and in the therapeutic relationship.

The session opened the door, over time, to questions about herself: *Mature little girl that I am.* She *still* played the role of "mature little girl," but is that what she really *wanted*? It opened the door to questions about *other* losses, such as hopes and dreams she'd always had. As she came to value herself more, she started to challenge herself—would she *really* want a child with someone like Gary? Now in her forties, she figured that letting him go would mean never having kids at all.

It opened the door to questions about the therapy relationship. She realized she was opening up, trusting me more, experiencing painful feelings in my presence—this was all rather exposing. It meant encountering hidden parts of herself. Normally, her go-to was to *take care of* others, but to feel *taken care of* by others? To feel understood by me? That was much harder. It meant facing her vulnerabilities.

And throughout the therapeutic work, she would confront many losses, and the feelings that went alongside.

Indeed, loss is inevitable in the human experience and essential for growth. We feel it from the start and throughout our lives. Viorst opened her book *Necessary Losses* (1986) with, "We begin life with loss. We are cast from the womb without an apartment, a charge plate, a job or a car. We are sucking, sobbing, clinging, helpless babies" (p. 21).

When We Lose Illusions About the World and Ourselves

A Changed Worldview

Some time ago, a Canadian soldier and his sister, who were both interested in educating the public about military life, trauma, and psychological health, agreed to be interviewed for *The Trauma and Mental Health Report*, an online magazine I edit (Bick, 2011a, 2011b).

Having served in Afghanistan for nine months with the Forty-Eighth Highlanders, a Scottish-Canadian brigade, the corporal's return to civilian life was fraught. He described his emotions as bottled up for so long, suddenly exploding inside. And his homecoming to Canada came with a laundry list of unwelcome symptoms: "I used to be a very sound sleeper, but I now awake suddenly to the smallest of noises. I am so used to being alert, focused, and prepared to react at all times" (Bick, 2011a).

While on a visit to downtown Toronto with his fiancé—the two of them were celebrating a national holiday—fireworks were set off nearby, and his heart began to race uncontrollably. He felt as if he was right back there, patrolling the streets of Afghanistan.

Perhaps the metaphor of emotions "exploding inside" is apt. One of his more disturbing experiences overseas was a near miss, an explosion (Bick, 2011a). He recalled:

> At one point I was assigned to a specific checkpoint for about a month where I checked the IDs of every individual who passed by. My position was later taken over by an American soldier. After being relieved for only about an hour, I was informed that a bomb had gone off near the checkpoint, and the American soldier who took over my position was killed. It is almost impossible not to question: What if . . .

Traumatic experiences do make us question. And they *raise* questions, questions about our safety and security in the world: *What if that were me?* Questions about fairness: *Why me? . . . Why not me?* Questions about our place in the world—luck, fate . . . do we control our own lives? Questions about ourselves, personal responsibility, and our role in the way events unfold: *Did I cause that? Was I somehow at fault? Should I feel at fault?*

Over many years, psychologists Daryl Paulson and Stanley Krippner worked clinically with combat veterans returning from Vietnam. They found a *changed worldview* in so many of the men and women they talked to. "The ever-present memory and realization of war, forever operating on both conscious and unconscious levels, has taken the joy and sparkle from many lives" (2007, p. 27).

Loss of trust, loss of faith in others, loss of innocence—a world now seen as unpredictable, as undergoing constant, threatening change, where death is understood as an overshadowing truth. For many trauma survivors, their expectations of reality have changed forever.

And the illusions we typically live with? *I'm safe; people are good; death is far off in the distance.* They're illusions that normally embolden us, ease us through our days. But as Paulson and Krippner explain, for veterans who've seen death and suffering firsthand, who've lived alongside danger and insecurity, they're words that ring hollow. Having witnessed the unfairness of death, there's a shift in how many survivors view the world, in their sense of life's purpose, direction, and meaning. For them, there is now a disillusionment that runs deep. Paulson and Krippner (2007) wrote:

> For the modern infantryman, like his predecessors, life will never again be the same. No longer can he dismiss death as an event far in the future. Even if he survived the war, he would know always that death is but an instant away. No matter where he is, no matter what job or position he may hold, no matter whom he marries, no matter how financially secure he is, he will always know, deep in his heart, that life on this earth holds no permanence for him. (p. 87)

A Changed View of Self

For the psychologist who penned those words, a changed worldview was a personal one too. Decades earlier, Daryl Paulson had served as a U.S. marine in Vietnam. In his moving account, *Haunted by Combat* (Paulson & Krippner, 2007), he recalled how—like the Canadian corporal described earlier—the return home was in some ways harder than the period spent overseas: "During this time, I had to face the dark side of my personality, the side that had participated in the killing and maiming of other human beings and had witnessed the brutal killing of friend after friend" (p. 102).

For Paulson, and so many like him, an admission that he was suffering emotionally felt like an admission of weakness. Having had a bad therapy experience years earlier with a psychiatrist who seemed cold and uncaring to him, Paulson struggled with trust. And it took a long time to build a solid, collaborative relationship in psychotherapy, one that could contain all the feelings he felt plagued by:

> I had to experience the war all over again; this time, emotionally, I had to face the various combat situations I had been holding in. I had to acknowledge that I had killed and had done it with great satisfaction. . . . I realized that had I been a German soldier in World War II, and had I been asked to

gas Jewish prisoners, I unquestioningly would have done so. I would have justified it, thinking our leaders know what is best. (p. 102)

Paulson came face to face with a profound guilt about what he'd done, about the harm he'd caused others, and about how willing he'd been to do it. In other words, he confronted aspects of *himself* he'd never faced before. And so, not *only* did he experience a change in how he viewed the world, but also *his* place *in* it.

This happens often in trauma. Thrown into overwhelming situations, confronting danger, fear, and a wish to endure, we encounter aspects of ourselves we've never known. In the interest of our own survival, we harm others, we are self-serving, we betray.

And this doesn't just happen on the battlefield. We see this all the time in traumatizing homes where siblings are pitted against one another. We see this in bullying situations in schools and online. Teenagers step aside—they're bystanders—as peers are brutalized. We see this in divorce scenarios, where otherwise reasonable people now behave with contempt toward those they used to love.

To recover from trauma, Paulson would mourn the loss of who he *thought* he was: the loss of illusions about himself, how he used to see his place in the world. He would also mourn the loss of *the him* that once was—aspects of himself that had changed forever. And he'd come to accept painful truths: parts of himself he'd never before recognized, unflattering as they were.

His view of the world would have to change, yes. But his view of *himself*, and his place *in* the world—that would change too.

A case comes to mind of an older woman whom I worked with. Isabelle struggled a lot in her relationships with her grown kids, all of whom worked in the family business. The children complained Mom was impossible to please— a nightmare since Dad died, depressed. She complained she felt sidelined, irrelevant. She would become ill-tempered with them, critical of their business choices, finding fault with their life partners.

A decade earlier, Isabelle's husband had died peacefully in his sleep. She spoke respectfully of the marriage. I heard nothing untoward or unusual, although it all sounded rather detached. They'd married young, and her husband had worked hard. Together, they'd built the business from scratch, a wholesale broadloom-carpet company.

There are some clients we form especially close connections to, and it's not always clear why. Isabelle was demanding, irritable, rigid. . . I liked her. In me she saw a "son" of sorts. But unlike her actual kids, I was free to take her perspective, to empathize, without the burdens of her motherly criticism—I had it easy. In her, I saw a "grandmother" of sorts—my own had died just a couple of years earlier, and we'd been close.

A telephone call from Isabelle's youngest son—he was worried Mom was still depressed—led to a meeting with the two of them, focusing mostly on her safety. And toward the end of the session, as her son put on his jacket, while Mom made a quick trip to the restroom, he shook his head in utter frustration, muttering under his breath, "The way she talks about Dad, you'd think he blew sunshine out his ass."

He was right. In front of her son, Isabelle had idealized the relationship with her husband, putting him on a pedestal. It was all too disingenuous. And in later sessions, as we would discuss the marriage more deeply, her feelings toward her husband would come across as more complicated than she'd previously let on.

And right there, we came up against Isabelle's struggle to mourn. The year before her husband's death was a difficult one. He'd made some poor business decisions, and their carpet company seemed to be failing. Their marriage suffered, and he was very hard on the kids, all of whom had joined the business. Within months of their youngest child moving out, her husband died of a heart attack in his sleep. He'd been a lifelong smoker, sixty pounds overweight—still, her immediate thought was, "I caused it." The truth was—and she'd never confessed this to anyone before—for years she'd been experiencing the disturbing, intrusive thought: *I wish you would die.*

A kind-hearted person, it wasn't like Isabelle was typically in the habit of wishing anyone dead, much less her husband. Every few weeks, the unsettling thought would come to her, although she would try to put it out of her mind.

To her, his death was a punishment. Her wish had somehow killed him, and she judged herself harshly for it. And now I understood—it made sense to me why a decade after his death she was *still* struggling. It wasn't really the loss of her *husband*. Losing *him* wasn't what she still had to mourn.

Like in Paulson's case, for Isabelle to recover from the loss, she would have to mourn the loss of illusions about *herself.* She would have to mourn the loss of who she *thought* she was—who she once was, and who she imagined herself to be.

There were painful truths she would have to accept about herself: her lingering anger at her husband for giving her what amounted to a disappointing marriage, and her anger at herself for staying in it. She chose, at age seventeen, against her parents' wishes, to marry a man who could take her away from her traumatizing family. But in the end, as she realized, perhaps her parents had been right. He *was* a rather bad match.

And the effects on the children of her unhappy marriage—this too was painful to realize. She was tough as a mother. She would come to recognize that her kids experienced her, at times, as hard to take. In fact, she'd been unhappy in the relationship for years. Her "wishing him dead" was, after all, an expression of that unhappiness. And the part of her that would take it out on her kids—this was painful for her to accept.

She would have to face, as well, the loss of the marriage she'd always wished for—a dream that died long ago, but had never been recognized.

Her losses went way beyond her husband's death: lost aspirations, lost ways of viewing herself. Having married young, her way of characterizing much of her relational life would change. How she saw her past, and her role in how it unfolded—these would change too.

In time, adopting a more nuanced view opened a door: Growth came with a more integrated, honest view of herself, with accepting parts of herself she hadn't known. And with it came the possibility that she might, eventually, forgive herself.

How We Undermine Mourning

Throughout this book, I discuss avoidance of the past. Many people with trauma histories struggle to speak of overwhelming experiences and memories. They cut off unmanageable feelings. With family and friends, many have enduring difficulty with vulnerability.

In Chapter 3, I pose the question, What underlies avoidance in trauma? Recall that first, I consider the role of *protection*. Some of our stories are too frightening to deal with directly. In some families, recounting painful memories or experiences is unacceptable. When we fear our own past, avoidance is a way of protecting ourselves. And when expressing our feelings can disturb or alienate those closest to us, avoidance is a way of protecting others and our relationships with them.

Secret keeping, resistance to personal storytelling, loyalty to family or tribe—these all protect ourselves and those closest to us from painful truths.

Recall also in Chapter 3, when discussing what underlies avoidance in trauma, I consider the role of *suppression*. Culture and history suppress trauma narratives. How we understand our own experiences, how we narrate them is always within a context.

Do we label our own suffering as traumatic? It depends on the time and place we live in. Culture and history support, shape, and silence trauma narratives. We're often unaware of subtle forces acting on us. In response to cultural expectations, we minimize and forget about unspeakable life experiences; we refrain from engaging in acts of remembrance, from incorporating our past into our personal identities, from owning our history.

But there's another important thread I haven't picked up yet. The silencing of traumatic experiences, feelings, and relationships is part of a larger prohibition. It's one that runs through modern Western culture. It permeates values, aspirations, ideology. I raise it now, in this chapter, because it has direct bearing on trauma and mourning, on the expression of feelings that mourning requires.

I am speaking here of the long shadow cast by the "positive thinking" movement, both as ideology and discipline. Advertised as a boon to health, happiness, and success, its impact has been profoundly felt and decidedly mixed.

The Downside of Positive Thinking

Why the concern? Mainly, because "positive thinking" is an ideology that blocks honest and open expression of suffering. It places an embargo on so-called negative thinking and feeling.

The roots of the movement can be traced to "New Thought" philosophy, in mid-nineteenth-century North America. Science writer Barbara Ehrenreich (2009) outlines New Thought as a reaction to the harsh, punitive Calvinism brought by white settlers to New England. In the New Thought vision of such spiritual leaders as Mary Baker Eddy—who gained notability and wealth with the founding of Christian Science—God no longer would be hostile or indifferent. New Thought, according to writer Oliver Burkeman (2012), offered happiness and worldly success through the power of the mind, even going so far as to cure physical ailments. In this philosophy, negative thoughts were fiercely denounced.

But making the phrase *positive thinking* popular was to become the domain of Protestant minister Norman Vincent Peale (Ehrenreich, 2009). The publication of *The Power of Positive Thinking* in 1952 came with "ten simple, workable rules," including, "Whenever a negative thought concerning your personal powers comes to mind, deliberately voice a positive thought to cancel it out" (Peale 1952/1994, p. 28). Its cultural impact has been felt since, not just in the self-help cottage industry but in the rhetoric of business, religion, behavioral health, and pop psychology. For myriad gurus who identify with the ideology, "negative thinking" is still treated with disdain (Ehrenreich, 2009). (I should note that I'm *not* here speaking of cognitive-behavioral therapy's use of the term *negative thoughts*, an idea based on very different principles.)[4]

The influence on Western language of the positive thinking movement is felt in all corners. A survivor of breast cancer, Barbara Ehrenreich (2009) described the impact on the language of medicine:

> Positive thinking seems to be mandatory in the breast cancer world. . . . Even the word "victim" is proscribed, leaving no single noun to describe a woman with breast cancer. As in the AIDS movement, upon which breast cancer is partly modeled, the words "patient" and "victim," with their aura

---

4. Throughout this section, I critique the "positive thinking" movement and ideology. Note the term *negative thoughts* has also been used, at times, by practitioners of cognitive-behavioral therapy (CBT), creating unfortunate confusion. In fact CBT, properly conducted, is about helping people *make sense* of their thoughts and the impact they have. It's not about "eradicating" so-called negative thoughts. And so, in CBT, far better language for the same idea includes *dysfunctional, irrational,* and *unhelpful* thoughts. In fact, these are the terms many CBT therapists prefer to use, as they capture the treatment principles better. In CBT, the therapist draws the client's attention to *unhelpful* thoughts and to their influence on mood, as this builds the person's awareness on how their own mind works. The approach allows the client to reflect on both their passing and enduring thought patterns and the impact they have on them and their actions. As a method, CBT treats such thoughts empirically to help promote flexibility in the person's thinking and a more realistic, critical stance to their social world. Questions are posed to clients, such as, What effect does that thought have on you? How does it help or harm you? How accurate is it? As stated, CBT, conducted well, is about helping people *make sense* of their thoughts and their impact—not "eradicating" so-called negative thoughts. More on the topic can be found in Björgvinsson and Hart (2006).

of self-pity and passivity, have been ruled un-P.C. Instead, we get verbs: those who are in the midst of their treatments are described as "battling" or "fighting," sometimes intensified with "bravely" or "fiercely." (p. 26)

As "positive" as it is, positive thinking has had unintended consequences, with questionable benefits (Diener, Colvin, Pavot, & Allman, 1991; Ehrenreich, 2009; Kashdan & Biswas-Diener, 2014). My concern here? Worshipping the positive undercuts the expression of sadness. It's an approach that denies the authenticity of suffering.

By cutting off our painful feelings and thoughts, the ideology makes for a culturally sanctioned silencing of trauma—a suppression of the emotions, memories, and stories that haunt us most.

And the effects are to dampen mourning. Without access to painful feelings, how exactly are we to mourn? Do we mourn at all? Painting a portrait of a two-dimensional world, the ideology of positive thinking shuns ambivalence. It offers no space for the range of feelings accompanying trauma and the losses it brings. In *Trauma and the Avoidant Client* (2010), I wrote: "One client, who began going out on dates just weeks following the death of his wife of twenty-nine years, could not understand why his children 'didn't get it.' He was doing *fine*; they should stop 'making such a fuss' over him and every little decision he was making" (p. 81).

Cutting himself off from his own feelings, he closed the door on any expression of mourning. Attempting to stay positive, he worked hard to numb the pain. And this was someone who came to treatment claiming his biggest problem was he needed to stop being so negative all the time, asking me pointedly if that was something I could help him fix.

In trauma, maintaining a narrow "positive thinking" mind-set is tricky. We quickly come head to head with our "negative" sensibilities: sadness, shame, anger, betrayal, rejection. As in both Angelina's and Isabelle's cases in this chapter, these are feelings useful in recovery, necessary for authenticity and growth.

They're difficult feelings, yes, but they're *not* pathological. This distinction is an important one to draw in the wake of the positive thinking movement. When painful experiences are whisked away, when feelings are painted with broad brushstrokes as negative, they're construed as pathology. This has real-world consequences for clients (and therapists), who confuse sadness and mourning with a very different experience, that of depression.

When We Confuse Sadness With Depression

In *The Gate of Tears* (2015), rabbi-cum-activist Jay Michaelson explored painful emotions and their meanings, distinguishing between sadness and depression. Michaelson described how he'd struggled on and off with depression himself:

> It can be crippling, devastating, bleak. It makes it hard to live one's life. Subjectively, I experienced it as a dullness, a kind of lessening, or graying, of all emotion. Sadness, on the other hand, is part of being human. So is loss, pain, and loneliness. These are not veils in the way of feeling; they *are* feeling. They have their own hues and characters. Unlike depression, sadness does not worsen when one yields to it; it softens, teaches, makes way. And in the yielding is some of the quality of liberation itself. (p. xxi)

There is nothing inherently negative about sadness. Painful as it is, loss is necessary for growth and development. And *facing loss* is necessary to grow from trauma. But neither of these represents depression; neither is pathological.

As Judith Viorst (1986) has told us, we face loss and sadness throughout our lives: in death, being left, leaving others, moving on. Losses are necessary, in Viorst's view; we grow by losing and leaving and letting go.

In trauma therapy, painful feelings come up a lot. It can be no easy task, inviting clients to sit with the sadness of mourning. This is even harder when they've experienced depression before—when either they've gone through it personally or someone close to them has.

So often, people confuse loss and sadness with depression, especially when they believe they somehow *ought* to be happy. *I'm an optimist, I shouldn't feel sad.* There's even a sense that, not being the sunny one, they're letting others down. For those who have, in some way, experienced the darkness that is depression, feeling sad can be downright terrifying. They fear what may be in store. *Not depression again!*

I saw this with a client of mine, Connor, who started therapy because of his mother's unfortunate life situation. Although only in her sixties, Mom now required full-time care, having had a massive stroke just a couple of years earlier. A college professor, she'd collapsed in the middle of an economics lecture she was giving. Initial hope gave way to disappointment. In time, it became clear she would never recognize any of her family again: not her grandchildren, not her husband, not her son (my client). And, they were told Mom could live like this for years: alive, but mentally gone.

Connor's relationship with his mother was by no means perfect. For as long as he could remember, his mother had struggled with an eating disorder, along with several psychiatric hospitalizations for depression. She would openly share little. But during one of her inpatient stays, when Connor was still a teenager, he would learn the extent of it: the medications, the self-starvation, the suicide attempts throughout the years, the postpartum depressions after his and his sister's births.

The word he used to describe pre-stroke Mom was *relentless*. She'd take any opportunity to comment on food, fat, exercise, and women's figures. It was a point of irritation in the extended family. Few knew how mentally unstable she was, only how critical she was of "fat people," as Connor would say, mimicking the sour expression she'd pronounce the words with. And for his younger sister, who'd been heavy all her life, Mom's prejudice would drive her "up the wall."

Maybe it was his general composure, maybe it was how he'd tend to focus on the technicalities of his mother's care—the facilities, the visiting schedule, and so on—but when his mother finally did die, Connor's reaction surprised me as much as it did him. His voice-mail message was true enough to form: He explained matter-of-factly how he'd miss our meeting that week because of the funeral. But over the next few sessions, he would describe himself as a wreck.

His feelings shocked him. He thought they made no sense. For a time, he was sure he was getting depressed, just like his mother so often did. He wondered what all his distress was about. After all, her stroke—and all that went with it—was old news. It had been some time since she left her life behind . . . as an economist, as a professor, as a grandmother and mother. Anyone who knew her already thought of her as gone. Frankly, what was there left to grieve at all?

But he *wasn't* a wreck. And his feelings did make sense. Indeed, this was not depression but a reaction to loss. Yes, he'd long lost the intelligent mother he once knew, and the opportunity to say good-bye. The stroke had taken those already. But only now, in her actual death, could he recognize what he'd lost so much longer ago.

The sense that when you're at home you *feel* at home. This is how Connor would describe it—what was lacking, what he never had growing up. Precocious as he was, being the favored child was more of a burden than anything.

Even as a teenager, when he and his mother would have their political discussions, the mood was tense. They would go head to head. *You had to prove yourself.* Even once he got tenure as a professor, the prospect of a misstep, of an intellectual faux pas, scared him, especially in her presence. It had always been a pins-and-needles relationship.

And the sense of just how unstable he'd always felt in his childhood home, how insecure he'd always been with his own mom—that came to him only as we discussed his daughter. He realized that in his mother's death he felt some relief. His child was now out of danger. She wouldn't have *his* mother as a grandmother. There would be none of what his sister endured, none of the snide comments, none of the public humiliation. He hadn't before voiced this—his secret relief—but he recognized it. His daughter was out of the woods.

Still, the relief was only partial. With it came sadness.

Sadness for his sister, whose adulthood had been consumed by false starts, rejection, and mental illness. Sadness for his mother, whose intolerance of others was surpassed only by the harshness she'd visit on herself.

And, sadness for himself, because of the mother he had. Grief, because of the mother he didn't.

CHAPTER 8

Change by Way of Relationship

The Case of Nigel

Nigel found it all so embarrassing. *Humiliating*, he would say to me. He'd been covering up the relapse for weeks, hiding what went with it: the hotel costs, the strip clubs, the trips to the casino, the credit card charges. Everything had been kept a secret. And there was so much to be dishonest about.

He'd even managed to refinance the mortgage. He needed cash, sobering up for the day to look respectable at the bank, concealing the relapse, hiding the drinking from everyone, especially his wife and kids. Lying to them was the worst part, he would later tell me.

In the middle of the night, driving back to Toronto, he knew he was at the tail end of *this* bender. The escort he'd hired for the weekend was asleep, leaning up against him—too much wine. With record losses at the casino that evening, he was now beginning to panic. This was it; he'd reached the end. Somehow he had to stop himself.

And it wasn't like he'd never had relapses before. Some went on for months. The worst was in his early thirties, in law school, just before he moved to Canada from England. He was forced to take a year-long leave from his studies.

But since then, nothing like this. Since then, he'd been able to keep his drinking in check.

The rental car he was driving had no satellite radio. And the stations, along the flat, dull highway ride back to the city, were few and far between. Nothing to distract him from his thoughts.

Was it a suicide attempt? When I asked him that, weeks later, after discharge from the hospital, he said no, he didn't think so. But he couldn't recall *anything* from the accident. The collision had put the car in a ditch and him in the emergency room.

So then, what *did* he remember?

"Her *seatbelt*, I told her to wear a seatbelt, when she got in the car . . . and she did."

He leaned forward, pensive, absorbed in his own thoughts, maybe thinking just how badly he'd screwed up, maybe grasping just how narrowly he'd escaped. Hard to know. He had ducked a tragedy. The car had been totaled, but no one was fatally injured. Not him, not the nineteen-year-old in the passenger seat, the woman he'd paid to be with him for the weekend, the woman he described as two years younger than his daughter. By insisting on seatbelts, he'd saved her life, so to speak, even as his drunk-driving just as easily could have killed her.

And that was it. We would talk about it a lot over the next few weeks, but he would remember nothing else about the accident: darkness, until he woke up in the hospital; bruised, shaken, concussed.

I first found out about the accident by text. Nigel and I had been working together for just a couple of weeks. I was one of a handful of people he'd messaged from his hospital bed, a group thread, starting with three words: *I'm so sorry.*

And when I saw him next, soon after the fiasco, his wife Jocelyn joined us for the first few minutes of the session. A fashionable, well-dressed woman, her arm was draped so snugly around his neck and shoulders, I imagined he might choke. She was angry, hurt, yet grateful he wasn't dead. She had a lot to say:

Jocelyn, turning toward me, says, "It has to do with commitment. You don't do this kind of thing if you have a fundamental commitment to your family. Am I right?"

Nigel looks away, says nothing.

She goes on to describe recent events: how she's organized a three-month leave for Nigel with his partners at the firm, how she's gotten him to finally call back his Alcoholics Anonymous (AA) sponsor, how she's cooked up the lie they would tell their children.

Nigel shifts about in his chair, looking uncomfortable.

Jocelyn continues (still speaking to me, no longer touching him): "He does *his* thing, and you know what *my* job becomes? Disaster management. I'm the cleanup crew."

Nigel looks down at his hands, interlacing his fingers, saying nothing to defend himself or contradict her. He briefly looks out the window, seeming lost in thought. And then turns to her, saying she's right, and that he's sorry. There's an odd "little boy" quality to his tone, like he's "misbehaved."

Jocelyn turns toward me, looking frustrated, weary, and says, "I don't need 'sorry.' I need reliable."

Nigel relaxed into therapy over the next few weeks, which focused first on the crisis at hand: his distress at having disappointed his AA sponsor, his worry that the children would discover the truth, and his anxiety about the law society investigation soon to be under way. The task of recovery felt insurmountable.

It was a well-worn feeling. He'd been managing his drinking for years, since adolescence. And the connection between his and his mother's alcohol abuse was clear to him, the main reason visits abroad were so infrequent. Over the past two decades, they'd been back to England only a handful of times. Nigel had always made a point of keeping his children far from his past. They knew very little about him.

Adult Attachment Interview Meets *Star Trek*

A couple of weeks in, once the dust had settled, we spent a session on the Adult Attachment Interview (AAI), which as mentioned throughout, assesses the person's relational state of mind and orients them to think about their formative experiences with caregivers (George et al., 1996; Hesse, 1999; Steele & Steele, 2008). As I've said, early in the interview the client is asked to list five adjectives describing their childhood relationship with a given caregiver, going back as far as they remember. And then they're asked to go through the adjectives one at a time. They're invited to recall specific incidents or examples from personal history.

Volatile—that was the first adjective Nigel gave in describing his childhood relationship with his father. An electrical engineer, Dad left the family when Nigel was twelve, moving back to India, where he was from originally. I asked Nigel to recall specific incidents or examples, any memories that illustrate the relationship as volatile. He responded:

Yeah, right. Ehm, so . . . "volatile." (long pause) He had a short fuse, explosive. I recall getting spanked to the extreme. A lot. Sometimes for being cheeky, but sometimes just for getting *excited* about something. There was *so much* violence. (long pause) I'd get screamed at . . . punished for bringing friends home, when I wasn't supposed to, for breaking the rules. (pause) For *Star Trek*. (long pause) He *hated* my collection. I had an odd fascination with Star Trek. He called it rubbish, bloody stupid . . . American. I had everything. Collectibles, action figures, models, books, biographical sketches of the actors and the characters they played. That all set Dad off. It drove him mad, really, he hated it all. Sometimes he'd confiscate parts of my collection until I'd do my homework, maths especially. I was abysmal at that. Once a teacher, who was a miserable wretch —oh, she was just horrid—phoned home to complain about me. (pause) And Dad *smashed* my Star Trek collection. Broke everything. Threw it in the trash, and burned the books and everything else in the fireplace. I was screaming. I tried to stop him, but he wouldn't listen . . . I was screaming and pleading and crying . . . I wanted to die. (pause) And that was the end of it . . . I lost everything. (He looks out the window, pauses for a few seconds, turns back toward me, shaking his head.) Yeah . . . everything up in flames. (long pause) I sure didn't get any sympathy for that . . .

These are Nigel's words, how he recalled a defining moment between him and his father, one that had a painful impact. And there's a lot we can make of his words. But what I'd like to focus on instead is what he says *without* any words at all, what he says *nonverbally*, through his body language, and what I say with mine.

And it's not like there's much research to date analyzing how body language reveals itself during the AAI. The traditional coding system is based on verbal elements of the interaction—written transcripts—and analysis of what the interviewee *says*. In fact, coding of written transcripts can be done without seeing the interaction at all.

Yet so much of therapy is *wordless*. It happens in the *in betweens*, in the subtle physical movements, in the pauses, in the direction we face when speaking, in the eye contact, in the ways we relate to the space in the room.

This is important in trauma. Does the client choose to sit in the chair closest to the door, leaving themselves a quick exit route? Does the person hold a purse or jacket on their lap, keeping a safe object between themselves and the therapist? Or do they wear sunglasses indoors, keeping eyes and emotions neatly hidden? Does the client spend so much time mulling over an answer they've censored it beyond recognition?

Questions like these are the subject of a study that my colleague, psychologist Mirisse Foroughe, and I are conducting, along with graduate students Laura Goldstein and Kristina Cordeiro in the Trauma and Attachment Lab at York University (Cordeiro, Foroughe, Muller, Bambrah, & Bint-Misbah, 2017). We're studying parents in the community, many of whom have trauma histories, and we're looking at their nonverbal behaviors during the AAI—how these relate to functioning in the family, and to the parenting changes they make from treatment.

With Nigel, it was interesting—and I realized this only afterward, later that afternoon, while I was in session with a *different* client, someone placing great value on distance in personal space. I realized the contrast to my session with Nigel, just a little while earlier, and how oddly *close* Nigel and I had been sitting for much of the AAI, especially as he recounted stories that made him vulnerable and when I felt empathy toward him.

His hands were interlaced, elbows on knees, leaning forward for a good part of the session—I was mostly in the same position, leaning forward too. We couldn't have been sitting more than two or three feet apart—I *never* sit that close to clients. It was as though, at any moment, he might jump into my lap. My voice hushed, mirroring his, there was an intimacy to the interaction that, only afterward upon reflection, I found a bit unnerving. And although the session was a good one—he felt heard, understood—there was a nagging sense I later had of boundaries crossed.

Trauma Themes in the Early Work With Nigel

Boundaries would, in fact, become an important piece of our work together. Let's review here some of the themes so far. In his words, *I sure didn't get any sympathy for that.* He describes well the *invalidation* he'd experienced.

As I explain in Chapter 5, survivors of ongoing family-based trauma grow up in *invalidating environments* (Alexander, 2015; Linehan, 1993; Rizvi et al., 2013). The child's personal experiences are disregarded, leaving them unable to recognize or bear their own emotions. Feelings are minimized, dismissed, met with criticism or punishment. Confused about who they are, and what they've been through, they're left blaming themselves for the past, for their own suffering.

Abandonment was another important theme, from both his parents, but for different reasons. Not long after the *Star Trek* incident, his father left the family for good. Of course, Nigel was affected by the loss itself, but along with the loss came a sense of himself as culpable, as though he'd been too much trouble, and his dad had had enough. The silly hobby had *driven his father away*, and this was a burden Nigel would carry forward. It never dawned on him that, when Dad destroyed the collection, it was a *symptom* of his unhappiness and of a long-standing wish to leave; Nigel and his collection weren't the *cause*.

And the blame was quite explicit, too. His father's leaving was indeed considered Nigel's fault—his mother had told him so. Here we see invalidation, yes, but also *emotional abandonment* from the caregiver who stayed. His mother—born and raised in London—had been a schoolteacher, and from Nigel's description, it seemed she suffered from untreated anxiety, obsessive-compulsive symptoms, alcohol abuse, and depression. She'd had to stop working when her drinking made it impossible. After Dad left for India, Mom's condition became chronic; she was incapacitated.

As for *crossing boundaries*, this too was a lifelong theme. In the punishments he'd received as a child, there was no sense of proportion. From the explosiveness of father's temper to the false laying of blame, personal responsibility was turned upside-down. As I said, Dad's leaving was somehow deemed *Nigel's* fault.

When we're blamed repeatedly for the actions of another, it's hard to know where one person ends and the other begins. And the destruction of his beloved *Star Trek* collection—the story is *so* disturbing because of how *personally* Nigel identified with the smashed objects. Seeing them burn in the fireplace, he felt himself burn too. *I wanted to die. And that was the end of it . . . I lost everything.*

Of course, boundary difficulties continued for Nigel as an adult. Certainly the drinking was out of control, but so much else was as well. Even after his renewed commitment to sobriety, in his relationship with his wife, once again, we see personal responsibility turned on its head. There was a sense that *she'd* fix his troubles *for* him—his wife would take care of it all. In Jocelyn words: *He does his thing, and you know what my job becomes? Disaster management. I'm the cleanup crew.*

And boundary crossing would become a theme in *our* work, too. But it was only later, on reflection, that I realized it—only when a crisis occurred in the therapy relationship, when a rupture happened that, quite frankly, blindsided me.

The Relationship Goes Off the Rails: When Enactments Bring Ruptures

For a while, the boundary blurring wasn't all that obvious. If anything, for months Nigel came across as something of a "star client." He was motivated; he was active in his own recovery. We would talk about his personal past, his family, his relationship with Jocelyn, the wish to do right by his kids.

And it wasn't as though he was pretending, either. He was thoroughly "into" treatment. That mess he'd made, months earlier? He *never* wanted to repeat it again. The drunk-driving shenanigans would affect his law practice for a couple of years, before he would be cleared. As for his children, both of them were in university, studying psychology—they'd somehow managed to wrangle the true story out of Jocelyn's parents. Nigel was determined to improve things with his kids. He valued treatment; he used it.

He wrote in his journal, mourned losses, connected to feelings . . . Nigel would do it all. He would engage, he would self-reflect, he would cry on cue.

But with all this engaging and self-reflecting and crying-on-cue going on, it made it easy to miss the coffee deliveries.

There weren't many of them, just a few before the cancelations started happening. Nigel would show up to sessions with a coffee for himself and one for me. Normally, this would be something I would ask about, that's certainly basic enough. A gift of sorts . . . what does it *mean*? What *motivated* it? What does it mean if I accept, or if I don't? More important, what does it mean *to him*? These are useful questions. They relate to rejection, connection, reciprocity, the feeling that we *matter* to someone important to us—all important themes in trauma recovery.

Soon, coffees became scones. He would show up with two or three, the good kind. Same issue: a gift, easy enough to inquire about. But I didn't. And again, it's only on reflection that I realized all this coffee/scone gift-giving drama was going on at all. At the time, his simple "Wanna scone?" was only a quick exchange, after which he would launch into something else, typically something relevant or important to his family or past. And coffees and scones would fall off the radar.

What was going on? What were we *enacting*? Something was pulling me away from an *awareness of the relationship*, from noticing it, from being mindful of the interactions *between* the two of us.

Out of coffees and scones came missed sessions. When at last he had his secretary e-mail me to cancel, just before the appointment (*his secretary!*), this undoubtedly affected me. How indignant I must have become. I sent back a very crisp, professional, clinical-sounding e-mail—not mean-spirited, mind you—but one that had my most formal, not-so-warm, doctorly sounding voice; my professional signature at the bottom, degrees listed, he'd *clearly* gotten the better of me (again, I only recognized this in retrospect).

And what was his e-mail reply to me?

> Dear Dr. Muller:
> Are you *kidding* me?! Would you talk to your *children* that way?
> Nigel

And just like that, I faced the prospect of a therapeutic rupture.

Ruptures Always Blindside

When we speak of *ruptures*, we mean ruptures in the relationship, in the alliance between therapist and client. Where before it felt like a partnership, two people collaborating—with shared objectives, working toward improving the client's life—now the relationship has changed. It has been touched by conflict. As clinicians, we feel blindsided.

The client may think the therapist no longer understands them, doesn't "get it," isn't the same as before. Maybe the relationship now feels tainted or somehow ruined. They feel angry or hurt, viewing themselves as treated unfairly. Or, they fear getting "kicked out" of therapy. Or they go into a self-protective stance, hiding feelings of hurt from themselves, minimizing their disappointment in the therapist, or rationalizing away the relationship: *I never needed you anyway.*

And as clinicians, so often we experience the rupture as surprising, even shocking. There's a sense of it coming out of the blue, an anxious feeling that, where everything had been going so well, now the relationship hangs by a thread. Therapists may respond, at first, with confusion or defensiveness, convincing themselves the client *"went crazy" for no good reason.*

But when we find ourselves using pejorative language to describe the client—language reserved for unpleasant arguments with loved ones—there's no doubt we've been activated. Something has gotten our goat. And our job is to understand it and how it has played out in the therapeutic relationship.

Ruptures Come From Enactments

In *Attachment in Psychotherapy* (2007), psychologist David Wallin took a close look at the psychotherapy relationship. He described the *enactments* that occur in treatment, writing that the relationship is influenced by both therapist and client. For both people, something from inside has been triggered and acted on, something out of awareness, something emotionally compelling.

Psychotherapy is, of course, highly interpersonal. In countless ways, both members of the partnership affect one another. Wallin noted, for example, that the client's words "pull us in or push us away, open us up or shut us down, make us comfortable or heighten our anxiety" (2007, p. 270). And naturally, we affect the client similarly. The therapeutic relationship is co-constructed.

But even more complicated, therapists and clients bring their attachment orientations—their lifelong patterns of relating to close others—to the treatment relationship, along with their individual and family histories. When enactments occur, something painful has been provoked, not just in the obvious reality of a two-person interaction but also in the ways personal histories, internal experiences, and vulnerabilities collide. Wallin wrote: "Enactments are the scenarios that arise at the intersection, so to speak, of the unconscious needs and vulnerabilities of the patient, on the one hand, and the therapist, on the other. . . . In an enactment, aspects of the therapist's representational world—the legacy of her original attachment experiences—are unconsciously activated and lived out. Exactly the same is true for the patient" (2007, p. 271).

This is why we *fall into* enactments. They're surprising, precisely because they operate out of awareness. Born of our needs and insecurities, they engage us fully, provoking all the ways we protect ourselves from hurt and painful feelings.

A nerve is touched, and we get drawn in, acting *reflexively* instead of *reflectively*. And when the therapy relationship is suddenly in jeopardy, when we find ourselves blindsided by unexpected conflict, we can bet that some drama has been enacted, unconsciously, in the space between therapist and client.

Enactments happen often in trauma therapy. Sometimes they play out "abuse dynamics," where they replicate interpersonal themes relevant to the trauma. Psychiatrist James Chu (2011) explained:

> In the typical crisis of a reenactment of the relational dynamics of early abuse, patients feel angry, disappointed, and/or betrayed by therapists' responses (or lack of responses). In this situation, patients once again feel abused and may act abusively toward therapists or themselves; therapists feel cast in the role of abuser, may feel abused by their patients, and have certainly failed as the hoped-for-rescuer and feel—at best—like the indifferent bystander. (p. 167)

Enactments often play out abuse dynamics like these. But in my experience, the *way* they play out is often quite subtle. As I mentioned, enactments happen out of awareness, so they might go on for a while before the therapist notices them. That is to say, they can be hard to spot.

For example, think about the person who repeatedly comes to sessions, their list of prepared questions in hand, yearning for guidance—seeking a guru of sorts—putting the clinician up on a pedestal. The client's lifelong pattern of low self-esteem interlocks with the therapist's need to feel smart, wise, helpful, or heroic. And this pattern is then reenacted, sometimes for months, hindering change.

In this example, I say the enactment is subtle because, at first glance, therapist and client *look like* they're doing therapy. The clinician is being kind and curious, the client is listening to good advice, and they're talking. But the enactment is happening out of awareness. The two have fallen into a pattern that meets the unconscious needs of them both: the client's need to depend on someone "smart and strong," and the therapist's need to take on that role.

Together they play this out, with each other—a pattern the client has repeated often with others in their relational world. And in the end, the therapy misses the mark. It's a lost opportunity for growth and development.

Enactments and Ruptures Are a Big Deal in Trauma Therapy

Why care so much about enactments and ruptures? Because if we don't, the therapy can quickly spiral downward.

As in Nigel's case, we see that a good treatment alliance can become threatened. And if left unaddressed, what happens is dropout. There are so many ways therapists can fumble a tense moment, when the relationship is on the line. And the result? Clients, after months of effort, now find themselves seeking help anew, scratching their heads about what happened at all.

This is all-too-common in the field of trauma, and it's a problem. It feels defeating for the person who's had multiple on-off trauma treatments, numerous false starts. They've gone through a laundry list of therapists, the work ending prematurely and painfully each time, for vague reasons, with loads of misunderstanding and hurt feelings.

This easily could have happened with Nigel. At precisely the moment when he e-mailed me his response—*Would you talk to your children that way*—just then I might have answered with defensiveness or irritation. Or I might have become contrite, anxious, or desperate, or conflict avoidant, none of which would have been helpful.

Enactments are inevitable. What therapists *do* with them . . . that's what makes all the difference. In his writings, psychoanalyst Michael Franz Basch (1980) underscored this point. When treatment doesn't work out, it's so often because something has soured the relationship. In fact, Basch pointed to the therapist's inability to navigate relationship challenges as the most common reason for unsuccessful therapy.

But enactments shouldn't just be "managed." True, if left unchecked they can lead the treatment off a cliff. But as therapists, we need not fear them. In fact, as I said, we step into enactments. They're part of the work. The trick is to *use them* well, to see them as *therapeutic opportunity*. And when enactments are used well, they become moments of growth. The most damaging thing about trauma is how it affects the person's way of relating, how they interact with the social world is handicapped, touching every facet of life. As a client of mine used to lament, *people are everywhere!*

In James Chu's words: "The prominence of disordered attachment in the etiology and expression of trauma-related disorders suggests relational issues must have a central role in the psychotherapy of these disorders" (2011, p. 75).

The therapeutic relationship presents a live opportunity where the client can face relational patterns that hinder them most. When therapists *use* the enactment, they shine a spotlight squarely on the relationship, inviting the client to look at a real moment between them: *What happened just then? What happened between the two of us?*

And when we face conflicts in the relationship, and do so mindfully, collaboratively, with curiosity, without defensiveness, it represents a here-and-now possibility for interpersonal healing.

Enactments come from the colliding vulnerabilities of both client and therapist, so they have currency. There's something on the line—when conflict enters the relationship, or when there has been a rupture, tension and anxiety are palpable, as is a sense of risk. The whole therapy could go under. But that's precisely what makes times like these so powerful.

When there's a feeling of treading on thin ice, the moment is risky, but memorable. For people who have lived with mistrust and betrayal, conflicts like these are frightening, painful, even triggering. But they bring about remarkable opportunity for change, a chance to influence long-standing patterns.

From Enactments and Ruptures to Repairs: It's *All About* the Repair

How do clients benefit from the *repair* of a ruptured alliance? When it goes well, the change is tangible, sometimes profound. Most of all, they come to appreciate that relationships *can* be repaired, that conflict doesn't mean game over, and that resolving conflict in a relationship can enrich it.

For those who have lived through interpersonal trauma, this lesson certainly isn't obvious. The idea that *struggling* is part and parcel of *being* in relationships . . . this idea is foreign and, for some, unfathomable.

And this is why moments like these make the treatment so tenuous. For many, conflict goes hand in hand with abuse, rejection, and loss, with the end of the relationship. They avoid it at all costs.

As therapists, the work of repair begins with *noticing* what's going on around us: that we've stumbled into an enactment. "Noticing" may seem self-evident—how can you deal with something unless you know it's there? But spotting an enactment is easier said than done. It means paying close attention, to ourselves—especially our internal experience—to the client's experience, and to the relationship.

Noticing Enactments Requires a Self-Reflective Stance: Looking Inside

How can we tell we've stepped into an enactment?

There are, of course, telltale signs: One client takes much more energy than the rest, more of our time, more emotional investment; and they pick up on our resentment, feeling yet another rejection in their lives. Or, the person cancels and we feel relief, a secret hope they'll somehow disappear. Sadly, we let the therapy fizzle out, forgetting about them, as many do, replicating a painful pattern for them.

Or—different case—the client cancels and we feel wracked with anxiety, a need to "check up" on them. And we do just that—we check up on them more than necessary, disempowering them in the process, leading them to feel incompetent, yet again. Or, we feel guilty for routine confrontations—*Was I too hard on her last session?*—and repeatedly let the client off the hook. Or, we reduce fees for someone who doesn't need it, making exceptions when there's no exceptional financial need, feeling manipulated in the process.

In hindsight, we see how all of these were enactments. But in the moment's drama, therapists can get pulled in. And even common patterns like these, when we're living them in real time, can be hard to recognize. As I say, enactments happen out of awareness; they're often subtle.

And they're hard to notice, because seeing them means seeing aspects of *ourselves*, our needs, our wishes. It means facing our insecurities. It means accepting, even embracing, our vulnerabilities.

The idea that we've been drawn into an enactment requires openness, a certain nondefensive stance, a willingness to admit we've gotten it wrong. Do we feel *duped*? Or like we fell for some "trap"? Maybe we've been getting it wrong for a while now. Catching our errors, acknowledging that, say, we've crossed boundaries when we should have "known better"—this is necessary, or we won't notice the enactment at all.

And especially for therapists who have been in the field for a while, getting blindsided feels humbling: *What on earth was I thinking? Accepting scones? . . . Seriously?!* But beating up on ourselves doesn't get us far. Facing an enactment means setting aside self-reproach and instead *looking inside* to understand ourselves.

It means, as psychologist Peter Fonagy would say, *mentalizing* our own experiences and those of the client (Allen & Fonagy, 2006; Allen et al., 2008). When we're in different states of mind, when our vulnerabilities are provoked, we can experience and feel things very differently. Adopting a self-reflective stance is about looking inward, with curiosity and flexibility, without judgment. It means seeing that the client stirs feelings in us or prompts us to behave in certain ways.

In different contexts, we often find ourselves in different mental states. And when we're curious about our own motivations, we're open to the idea that, as therapists, *we get triggered*. Something about this client, something about me, something about the way we relate . . . with an open-mind, we ask ourselves, what about *me* got activated? Why *then*? What was going on for me that I felt that way? Or, what's going on for me that I'm saying/feeling/doing things I normally don't?

Or, how did *my* anxieties, fears, or hang-ups activate the *client*? And in the process, not only are we open to finding our errors, but we look for them. The position is one of radical exploration.

This is tough to do, but important nonetheless, especially when working with trauma survivors. With Nigel, making sense of what happened between us meant recognizing that, in subtle ways, we had been breaking boundaries all along, right from the beginning.

Recall that, although we had been working together only a couple of weeks, I was one of a handful of people he messaged from his hospital bed. In fact, he sent a *group thread*, an oddly *familiar* thing to do. And recall our unusually close seating, where we *leaned toward* one another during the AAI, and then the "coffee deliveries," and then the cancellations that came after.

To understand my part in our relationship, I had to appreciate that, bit by bit, we had been crossing a line, from the start. And that I was playing a role.

But what makes this an *enactment*? As I mentioned earlier, boundary crossing was something Nigel saw a lot, throughout his life. From the false laying of blame (it was deemed his fault that Dad had left) to the psychologically cruel punishments received as a child, boundaries were confusing to him. And he often used their blurring to his advantage, somehow getting Jocelyn, for example, to not only forgive him but also dig him out of the mess *he* created, despite her expressed resentment.

As for me, I came to recognize how I had been drawn in. There was a charming quality, a "little boy" eagerness, if you will, that was endearing and made Nigel gratifying to work with. It made it hard to notice that boundaries were being crossed at all. Maintaining his status as some kind of "special" client was motivating not only for him but also for me.

And for Nigel, while the closeness that came with crossing boundaries may have felt good in the moment—*Dr. Muller accepted the gifts I brought him*—as a trauma survivor loose boundaries are triggering. They represent a lack of safety. After all, how can you tell which lines will be crossed next? And when there's a lack of safety, the therapy quickly unravels.

But before *any* of this could be addressed *with* Nigel, before we could look at how this theme—played out with me—was a familiar one in his life, an important relational piece had to happen.

Unless and until the therapist *validates* the client's experience, no amount of exploration, unpacking, or direct discussion will help.

Relational First Response: Validation

As I've said, trauma survivors, especially those who experience intrafamilial abuse, grow up in *invalidating environments*. Psychologist Marsha Linehan (1993) highlighted the damaging effects. Invalidation undermines one's understanding of personal experience and self-knowledge. It makes people doubt their own interpretation of their motivations and actions.

When feelings are disregarded in the family of origin, it's difficult for people to recognize or bear their own emotions. And when painful experiences are minimized, dismissed, or met with criticism or punishment, people end up misunderstanding what they lived through. They struggle with who they are.

Describing Linehan's treatment approach, psychologist Shireen Rizvi and colleagues explained that such an environment "invalidates an individual's communication of internal experiences, including emotions . . . the expression of private emotional experiences is not tolerated" (2013, p. 74).

As I explain in Chapter 5, invalidating environments are confusing. People end up second-guessing their own memories, doubting what they know to be true, disregarding themselves. They discount their own traumatic experiences and mistrust their own self-knowledge.

And because their personal experiences are dismissed, they grapple with interpersonal boundaries. When you're repeatedly told your subjective world is wrong, it's hard to know who "you" are, much less where you (and others) begin and end.

As therapists, when we *validate* the client's experience, we listen, we empathize, we don't judge. Regardless of whether it makes sense on the face of it, we pay attention to the person's subjective experience. We stay close to the here and now, we try to understand what they're feeling in the moment.

We take a leap of faith that there's a reason the person is feeling that way, even if it's confusing to us right now. And we pay attention to the client's expressed emotions, conveying an attitude that values their subjectivity, clarifying our best understanding, to the extent that words can ever capture experience.

Why is this so important? And what does validation have to do with repair, with addressing therapist-client conflicts? Why is it necessary to validate the client's experience, following enactments and ruptures?

For one thing, if the person doesn't feel validated, we hit a wall. As I mention above, unless and until we *validate* the client's experience, we go no further. There's no exploration, discussion, or anything else to be had.

Why is this so? Because now, during conflict, the relationship doesn't feel safe. And so, this is an especially tenuous moment in the drama of enactment-rupture-repair. This is where the treatment can really go south. If the client can't *re*-find a sense of safety in the relationship, they will drop out, or "take a break," or find dozens of reasons to stay away.

But validation isn't meant to be applied strategically, manipulatively. *Validate, and the client will get back on board.* No, validation has to come from a *genuine* place. There has to be an authentic motivation on the therapist's part to "get it," to be curious about their own role in the conflict—how they may have triggered the client—and to be open to the client's personal experience, even if the therapist thinks it's different from what they'd feel in similar circumstances. If validation feels false, if the therapist is only placating the client, that will come across.

The challenge is to authentically understand the client's experience. And this requires a willingness on the part of the therapist to be nondefensive, to be vulnerable, to reflect on, for example, *How did my words or actions hurt my client?* or, *How did I get drawn into that . . . what was going on for me?*

When we validate genuinely, this is important because it strikes a chord. It takes the client's experience seriously, and for many, that's not a given. So often in trauma, especially within the family, the pain is compounded by others' responses. When abuse disclosures are met with minimization, dismissiveness, or worse—outright denial or victim blame—the person is left disheartened and retraumatized.

Recently, psychologist John Briere and colleagues studied adults with histories of childhood sexual abuse (Godbout, Briere, Sabourin, & Lussier, 2014). Some had parents who responded, long ago, to the abuse disclosure with supportiveness, and some had parents who responded unsupportively. The researchers found that parental response made a big difference in terms of later attachment security and psychological symptoms. And incredibly, those whose parents had responded supportively did about as well as those who hadn't been abused at all.

Validation, if communicated honestly, paves the way to mutual exploration. It expresses curiosity about the person's subjective experience. It says their experience matters.

But validation doesn't mean *collusion*, either. And this part is also important. It may feel supportive to *agree outright* with the client, with their attributions, projections, or interpretations. But when we simply collude, we undermine the possibility of change and growth, we miss an opportunity.

And where conflict in the therapeutic relationship is concerned, when we collude we let the client off the hook. In an attempt to be supportive, we agree with them out of hand, and that undermines the possibility of learning from the conflict, from understanding what took place between us, in the space between therapist and client.

A client's *worry*, for example, that when I went on vacation I stopped caring—this can be seen as entirely valid. It may, in fact, have come from impressions I gave in the last session: my becoming easily distracted, feeling impatient to get away already, and so on. Her *worry* that I stopped caring *is* valid. And I can take responsibility for my role, my contribution to feelings of abandonment, without resorting to collusion, without agreeing with the client's projections, with her worst fears. Her worry that I don't care doesn't mean I actually don't care.

And yet, her worry that I don't care *is* valid in its own right. By being distracted or impatient, I played a role in fueling her fears. To the client, those fears are compelling—they have currency.

As therapists, how do we respond? We use the moment well; we take the worry seriously. Together with the client, we examine it and its meaning in the therapy relationship. How did each of us impact the other? We can look at this together: *What did you feel when I said/did such-and-such? When you worried I stopped caring, what was the scariest part about that? And as we discuss this right now, what are you feeling?*

Validation opens the door to collaborative exploration. It makes it safe. It expresses curiosity, not judgment, about the client's feelings and experience. From that place, the person can relax into a more self-reflective stance. And then, we see a greater willingness in the client to consider the part *they* brought to the equation.

How did validation look with Nigel?

The e-mail he sent me: *Are you kidding me?! Would you talk to your children that way*—that served as something of a wake-up call, a reminder to pay attention, to notice the enactment going on in the relationship. I had become activated by him, and then I reacted, coming across as cold and distant. He was now hurt. The place to *intervene* was at the level of validation, in the here and now. I had to sit with his present experience.

And validation was front and center when I wrote my e-mail response, a simple acknowledgment that it was true—that *wasn't* how I try to talk to my children—and that I hoped he and I could speak about it, that it seemed something difficult or upsetting had happened between us.

When he came in, I picked up the thread. I worked within the subjective impression he had of being treated unfairly by me. It was clear he felt hurt. Without judgment, we looked at his personal experience: *What was it like for him to get my e-mail response? What was upsetting or painful about how I'd talked with him? And how did he imagine I talked differently with my children?*

With Nigel, it didn't take long for him to *re*-find a sense of safety in the relationship. In fact, as his hurt began to subside, as he now experienced me as decidedly unthreatening, a self-consciousness came about. Now, apologetic for having reacted as he did, he adopted a let's-put-all-this-behind-us attitude: *It's okay, really, it was no big deal.*

Without any map, without any sense of how one sits with conflict or tries to understand it, Nigel's default was to play ostrich. He and I had a strong foundation, and with him back to experiencing me as a secure figure, rather than cold and detached—like his mother, after Dad left—our recent conflict now felt altogether nonsensical to him.

But rather than ignore or minimize the conflict, the therapeutic work, as always, was about making meaning. Something painful had happened between us, and an opportunity now presented itself: to help him make sense of what had happened.

For many clients, this is hard to do but important to learn. Sticking with it is difficult. This is where *containment* comes in.

Providing Containment

In *Attachment in Psychotherapy* (2007), David Wallin included a good description of *containment*, looking at the concept through the lens of attachment theory and practice: "Parents who successfully contain their infant's unmanageable emotions with responses that convey empathy, coping, and appreciation of the child's intentional stance are engaged in a process of interactive affect regulation. Through this process, they are reinforcing their child's confidence in the attachment relationship as a safe haven and secure base" (pp. 48–49). Citing the work of psychoanalyst Wilfrid Bion (1962), Wallin also wrote:

"The supportive mother mentally contains emotional experience that the baby cannot manage on his own but manages to evoke in her" (p. 48).

Like a good parent, the therapist helps the client contain feelings that otherwise overwhelm—feelings that stem from the client, from the therapist, and from the interaction between the two.

When conflict erupts in the therapeutic relationship, this is distressing for people with trauma histories. Unless the therapist provides *containment* in situations like these, the client can't face the conflict or stick with it long enough to unpack what went on. Growth from relational conflict can't happen unless the person can bear to sit with it.

To provide containment, we must recognize the conflict—we name it. The therapist *frames* what's happening as conflict. It's one going on between the therapist and client. For example, I reflect out loud: *I think we're in the middle of a conflict*, or, *This is what conflict looks like*, or, *It seems we just had a conflict*. Depending on circumstance, I narrate what's going on in the room, I reflect, I notice what's happening *between us*.

Why? Because, doing so, in effect, comments on what this *isn't*. This isn't—or doesn't have to be—the end of the relationship. This isn't anger/hurt/fear about to become revenge or abuse. This isn't closeness about to become manipulation or coercion.

We also frame what's going on as conflict because, well, it's true. This *is* what conflict looks like. It looks and feels uncomfortable, messy, awkward; it's disappointing, especially when things had been going so well.

And when framed this way, with a reflective tone, with curiosity and interest, without judgment, noticing the interaction between us—*there's something going on here*—this feels containing to both client and therapist. I'm attentive to not come across as condescending—I don't want to come from on high. And I'm careful not to sound dismissive either, as if I'm viewing this as *just* some little conflict, like it's nothing to fuss over.

On the contrary, the conflict *is* important, not because, as feared, the feelings are destructive, but because, with experience, they become bearable. And along with the conflict comes an opportunity for mutual understanding. For those who have suffered interpersonal trauma, this way of thinking is by no means, easy, natural, or obvious.

And because the conflict is important, because the underlying feelings *can* become bearable, as therapists we're careful not to become contrite, not to adopt an overly apologetic tone. We resist the temptation to *rescue* the client from the tough feelings inherent in conflict or from the expectation that they'll take responsibility for their part. Rather, our attitude is one of curiosity. We want to understand what took place between the two of us. We both played a role. When therapists mistakenly rescue clients, they deprive them of an opportunity to sit with difficult feelings and work them through.

When we provide containment, we express confidence in the relationship to hold the conflict, as in *Figuring this out is hard, but it's something we can do together.*

Helping Nigel Unpack the Conflict: Mentalizing

What have we done so far? We've noticed the enactment, we've validated the client's experience, and we've provided containment. At this point, the lion's share of the work is done. The repair of the ruptured alliance is well under way.

The person has experienced, in real time, the sense that in relationships things go off the rails and then back on. Relationships aren't doomed to end in pain, disappointment, or hurt—they're not all created equal. For people who have suffered interpersonal trauma, this experiential knowledge is golden, memorable.

And with this experience, and a renewed sense of safety in the therapeutic relationship, there's now freedom to explore, an opportunity to gain understanding. This is the next step in getting the relationship back on track. The client is able to engage in it because they once again feel safe; the self-protective guard has come down.

When we help the client *mentalize*, we invite them to think about their motivations, their vulnerabilities, the state of mind they were in when triggered. Peter Fonagy explained that "we are mentalizing when we are aware of mental states in ourselves or others" (Allen et al., 2008, p. 2).

How does this look? With Nigel, I focused our attention on our relationship: *What about what I said triggered you most?* I adopted a collaborative, curious attitude about his painful emotions: *What was scary about feeling so angry toward me? What was liberating about it?* I invited him to consider the ups and downs of his emotional states: *What about that time, particularly, was so upsetting?*

I also encouraged him to reflect on his motivations, his intentions: *Thinking back on the times you brought me coffee, how were you hoping I'd react?* And I asked him to reflect on my motivations too: *After you read my e-mail, what did you imagine/worry I was saying to you? How did you feel about that?* I noticed when self-criticism or judgment got in the way: *Rather than scolding yourself, Nigel, for hating me, let's try to understand it . . . maybe you had a good reason for feeling that way.*

As therapists, we help the client look inside, to understand what motivated the conflict. We coach them through the challenge of authentic self-reflection. We adopt a conversational tone. True, the approach relies on the person's willingness to engage, but at this point they're also more open, and the therapist's genuine curiosity helps pique the client's. When such-and-such happened, what was going on for them? We help them grapple with what affected them so: *What triggered you most?*

And in opening up discussion like this, we adopt a position of *not knowing.* We have no idea where, precisely, the exploration will go, how long it will take, or what will come of it. But if the therapist sets the right tone—noticing the enactment, validating, containing—the exploration can go on for a while, productively, with surprising discoveries. It's a discussion that can come and go, one the clinician can bring back into the room when thematically similar, or contrasting, issues arise later in the treatment.

In the work that Nigel and I did, he realized that, on some level, he felt jealous of my kids. This was initially embarrassing for him to admit. But embarrassing or not, it was inescapable: *Would you talk to your <u>children</u> that way?*

This idea resonated for me. Our boundary violations felt more parent-child than anything else. I would come to realize my part in making Nigel my "special" client.

And while it became obvious to Nigel, almost immediately, why he would want to "make me" his father, so to speak (and what hurt when I failed to fill that role), what came weeks later was the connection to his *own* role as a father: how terrified he had felt to have children to begin with, and how worried he was that now, with the troubles he'd caused, his kids would be "messed up" for good.

And later still, how he would decide to come clean with them.

Yes, his kids already knew the truth about the relapse—they'd found that out months ago—but he'd never discussed it with them *himself.* There was a lot to say, and it was personal, about himself, about his family, how he'd turned out as he did. His own children knew almost *nothing* of his past. To Nigel, this was no longer alright.

The discussion would carry risk—he had no idea *how* they would react. But he wanted my help to prepare.

And we would walk through it together—not knowing how it would change the father he was . . . or shape the one he might become.

CHAPTER 9

Reclaiming Identity

Victor Revisited

Let's think back to the case of Victor from Chapter 6, the music student I worked with long ago. In that chapter, we looked at strained apologies, the impact they have on victims, and how rushing into forgiveness—or being pressured into it—is unhelpful and self-defeating for trauma survivors.

Here, we'll draw on that same case to anchor our discussion, but we'll focus on the question of *identity*—how identity is affected by trauma, how people struggle with how much to bring their victimization history *into* their identity, and how identity can be reclaimed through trauma therapy.

Recall that Victor, an undergraduate music major, had been drugged and raped as a teenager by his choirmaster, Scott. There was an investigation, trial, and eventually, a conviction. It all caused untold stress on the family, bringing a hasty end to their locally famous choir. It also divided the community: some believed in them, keenly voicing their support, but many shunned and bullied them.

Victor and his brother Martin were in conflict over the question of forgiveness (Scott, the choirmaster, had sent a letter requesting just that). Their parents were also divided in their opinions. Dad was much more inclined than Mom to grant the request—he wanted his son to forgive.

Victor felt very confused. His emotions were in turmoil. He saw an obligation to forgive and worried he'd disappoint his father if he didn't. He blamed himself for being in Scott's hotel room at all (where the rape had happened, during an out-of-town performance). He wished he hadn't brought all this misfortune on himself. And he struggled with questions of his own sexuality, wondering if the assault was, somehow, proof he was gay. Even though he had a girlfriend, a cellist in the music program, his sexual orientation was still unclear to him. Questions like these troubled him.

Part of my work with Victor was developmental. Now in his early twenties, in the process of considering what direction to take his future, Victor had anxieties that were, to some extent, similar to those of his peers. He faced many of the same questions of identity as his friends did, not knowing who he wanted to be, what he imagined for his life. In part, these were normative struggles.

Even some of his questions about his sexuality were normative. As I mention in Chapter 6, the developmental part of treatment was in helping him sit with the idea of *not knowing*: His sexual orientation might get clearer with experience, but he couldn't *make* himself know, or force the issue. It would take time.

And yet, much of the difficulty was a far cry from what we think of as typical anxiety, from the normative struggles seen in emerging adults. The treatment largely centered on the consequences of trauma. Having gone through an investigation and trial, where his motives were questioned at every turn, he was uniformly hard on himself and plagued by self-doubt, often serving as his own harshest critic.

When it came to intimacy, Victor struggled with trusting others. With his girlfriend, with his friends, he would turn discussion away from himself. Almost no one at university knew what had happened to him in high school.

Victor also blamed himself for the rape, justifying it as punishment for his sexual feelings, as if he'd somehow seduced the choirmaster into it, as if he was asking for it all along. He questioned himself a lot: his own intentions, his own judgment, his worth as a person.

To Victor, graduating high school meant leaving the past behind. More than anything, his first few years as an undergrad felt like a welcome reprieve.

When Trauma Dominates Identity

Victor felt robbed, cheated as a high school student. While his peers were "being teenagers," so to speak, he and his family were in the throes of the investigation and trial. With the therapist he was seeing then, he'd spend his counseling sessions talking about anything *but* the rape. And still, he felt it cast its long shadow. For a while—until the conviction—his parents' marriage became rocky. His family had to move homes, change schools.

Victor felt like the rape had taken over. It ruled his family, his life—it swallowed everything. It had shaken his parents' relationship with each other, his closeness with his brother, the friendships they'd had in their once tight-knit community. The investigation and trial had become a never-ending topic of conversation. The trauma had planted itself squarely in their home and held fast for the next half-dozen years.

And this is where the issue of identity comes in: Trauma has a way of dominating identity, by its overwhelming nature, by its tendency to take over. For so many, trauma *becomes* the person's story, the fundamental preoccupation, to the exclusion of all else. It controls the personal life narrative.

A client of mine once called herself an insect, entangled in the web of her trauma. It had worked its way into every nook and cranny of her life. Who was she, then, without the trauma to define her? What was left?

In his treatment book *Not Trauma Alone* (2000), clinical psychologist Steven Gold brought the issue of identity to the foreground, warning therapists that "many people with an abuse history are vulnerable to allowing their realities to be defined by others. Moreover, in the absence of a clear sense of self, an emphatic focus on abuse trauma can easily foster the perception that a history of victimization is the single most important thing about themselves, engendering the adoption of survivorship as a core aspect of their identities" (p. 50).

And how hollow it is for people to be defined, in totality, by their painful history. Given the many ways traumatic events affect peoples' lives, it becomes all too easy for the trauma narrative to become *the* dominant story, for it to represent the entirety of the person's identity. As Gold explained, "A focus on survivorship 'privileges' abuse experiences, casting them as uniquely decisive episodes in the person's life history. In the process, other possible influences on current functioning, including beneficial circumstances and inner strengths, as well as debilitating forces other than trauma, are subject to being obscured" (p. 49).

When we make trauma the defining life story—to the exclusion of all else—when we make it the dominant narrative, we disempower and diminish our clients. We take something away: the person's individuality, their humanity. We undermine personhood. We reduce a life to a series of misfortunes suffered.

What Is Trauma's Place in Identity?

Suffered right to the end! Few among us—other than the martyrs, perhaps—would want *that* as an epitaph. And yet, this book has been all about helping people face their painful histories, taking their suffering seriously, inviting them to open up in a safe context and make meaning of their experiences. Otherwise, how are they to live with the burden of a traumatic past?

Here, in this chapter on identity, my main caution is against excessive narrowness in *either* direction. Trauma is part of the story, but it's not the whole story. It shouldn't dominate identity, but it can't be sidestepped, either. Defining clients, in totality, by their trauma history *is* a problem. So too, is colluding with them as they kid themselves it was no big deal. A balanced, honest approach helps clients make sense of their past, in sincerity—it helps them *integrate* the trauma. How has their painful history affected their lives?

When trauma becomes the go-to, when it's used as a two-dimensional explanation for all that goes wrong, this limits people. It disempowers them. It closes them off from change and the possibility of growth and development. On the other hand, as I've discussed throughout, sometimes people rebuff the trauma perspective entirely. They dismiss their own past. They strenuously distance themselves from *victim* status—they want nothing to do with it.

The I'm-No-Victim Identity

Some years ago, there was an attempt to address wide discomfort with the term *victim* by replacing it with the more "positive" descriptor *survivor*. But this replacement label was hardly a solution.

Gold (2000) pointed out that the *survivor* term was adopted to avoid the connotation of helpless submission in *victim*. But as science writer Barbara Ehrenreich outlined in her compelling critique *Bright-Sided* (2009), this maneuver amounts to little more than rhetorical sleight-of-hand. All it does is replace one word for another.

As I note in Chapter 7, having undergone breast cancer treatment herself, Ehrenreich lamented the dishonesty she saw in the medical community, in their wide reluctance to use the term *victim*, tracing this to the positive thinking movement: "As in the AIDS movement, upon which breast cancer is partly modeled, the words 'patient' and 'victim,' with their aura of self-pity and passivity, have been ruled un-P.C." (p. 26).

In other words, call it like it is. Some things are dreadful, there's no dancing around it. Referring to victims as survivors makes it no better. And although in my own practice I've used the term *trauma survivor* for many years (I use it throughout this book), I try not to fool myself that *survivor*, somehow, has positive connotations. The wording makes little difference. Many of those who shun *victim* also shun *survivor*. Those struggling with the trauma perspective rebuff *victim*, *survivor*, and everything in-between. The uneasiness isn't with the wording.

It's with *vulnerability*. To identify with *trauma, abuse, posttraumatic stress disorder, survivor, victim* . . . it's a lot to ask of people. For some, it's all too much to take.

It can be very uncomfortable applying terms like *trauma* or *abuse* to ourselves. As a client once shouted at me: *When you call me a survivor, you're calling me a wimp!* Again, it wasn't about the word. Rather, this client struggled with how *vulnerable* it made her feel to face her trauma history.

Throughout, I've written about how self-deception is a common response to trauma. As I describe in Chapter 5, where I referred to the research of Berger et al. (1988), people often refrain from applying trauma terminology to themselves, despite histories that are, objectively speaking, clearly abusive. We see this when clients invalidate their own painful histories, minimize their past suffering, insist they don't deserve help for their "minor" problems, or try to figure it all out themselves without help.

Elsewhere, I've referred to the *I'm-no-victim* identity (Muller, 2009, 2010) seen in many who have experienced interpersonal trauma. I described this pattern in *Trauma and the Avoidant Client* (2010):

The words *trauma, abuse,* and *victim* all conjure up images of weakness and vulnerability. Phrases such as *survivor of abuse* have particularly negative connotations. And, emotional states associated with trauma, such as grief, sympathy, and self-pity, are all uncomfortable and contradict the dominant identity the individual has worked so hard to construct. In short, the client attempts to keep himself from being identified as a victim. (p. 45)

When Trauma Makes Its Way Into Identity

What, then, is trauma's place in identity? Clients struggle with this: how much to bring their victimization history *into* their identity. This is especially true early in treatment, when we see people expressing—often single-mindedly so—*I'm no victim.*

But trauma therapy affects people in wide-ranging, transformative ways. As psychiatrist David Scharff has quipped, psychotherapy is the "growth and development business" (Labriola, 1998). We've seen many examples of this throughout. And we see it in relation to identity, too, where over the course of treatment, rather than *dismissing* themselves and their painful history, clients become more accepting of their vulnerabilities. They come to appreciate that, while trauma isn't their *entire* story, it's certainly an important *part.*

In other words, how people understand their trauma shifts with treatment. And how they navigate their relationship *with* their trauma—and their evolving self-understanding—is a *process.* The changes are gradual, subtle, but they're meaningful. In time, clients adopt a more textured view of their past.

Shifts like these come about when therapists use a balanced, honest, trauma-informed approach—neither rushing into trauma revelations nor shutting the person down—validating painful experiences to the extent the client can accept, helping them tolerate and feel their painful emotions, such as the losses inherent in trauma, and using the therapeutic relationship as a vehicle for change. When therapists take an approach like this, clients come to *integrate* their traumatic experiences—making sense of them, understanding their impact—rather than trying to amputate them from their personal history.

And it's this kind of approach, precisely, that helps clients shift in how they view their painful past, to see it less narrowly, less rigidly, less either-or. Through treatment, the trauma is integrated *into* their life story. It's no longer dismissed, nor does it define them exclusively.

And if it isn't trauma, exclusively, that defines the person, what does? This is where thinking *beyond* the trauma comes into play.

Beyond the Trauma: Reclaiming

Trauma therapy gives people an opportunity to move beyond a restricted, static view of who they are. When treatment goes well, it arrives at a point where the client starts to *reclaim* important characteristics of *themselves*—qualities lost, for a time, to the trauma. For some, there's a sense of awakening. For others, they come to express ideas and feelings never before allowed. The person starts to permit for themselves—less apologetically, less ambivalently—what many of us take as a given. This is important where identity is concerned.

When therapy reaches this point, we see a newfound sense the client is starting to define conditions on their own terms. There's a tone of greater freedom.[11] It's not that everything is hunky-dory. With greater freedom come new realizations, new anxieties. For example, *He's such a jerk to the kids . . . What on earth am I still doing with him?* But with new realizations, the person can also see choices never before possible.

Reclaiming happens gradually, subtly, unevenly. Some clients come to it sooner than others, depending on their mix of psychological resources, such as self-esteem, smarts, talent, and fighting spirit.

In using the term, *reclaiming*, I don't mean something generic like feeling better, although that's certainly a piece of it. It does feel good to have fresh options. It represents an opening; it's future oriented. But reclaiming is more than just that. When trauma therapy goes well, people find facets of *themselves*—fundamental, human facets, qualities that had been lost for a time or were never much available at all. Let's look at these.

1. Columnist David Brooks distinguishes between two kinds of freedom: freedom as capacity and freedom as detachment. In Brooks's (2017) words, "Freedom as capacity means supporting people so they have the ability to take advantage of life's opportunities." Freedom as detachment, in Brooks's view, is giving people space; it's "based on the belief that people flourish best when they are unimpeded as much as possible." In the current context, when I refer to freedom, it's primarily freedom as capacity.

Reclaiming Intentionality

Most of us are fortunate enough to take basic *intentionality* for granted, as in, *I know my own experience as true, I know what I feel to be real, I know my own intentions*. This is an essential characteristic for agency and self-determination. We can't know our own minds if we lack intentionality. Certainly, if we live free—if no one forces us to believe black is white—we may even assume that *everyone* possesses this basic human characteristic, intentionality. *Do what you want to do, you're an adult*. But for many who have experienced interpersonal trauma, especially within the family, this may be more of a luxury than anything. Trauma takes from people their intentionality.

Referring to the *annihilation of intentionality* that occurs in some families, drawing on a great many parent-child observations, psychologist Arietta Slade (2005) documented that

> disturbed and abusive parents obliterate their children's experience with their own rage, hatred, fear, and malevolence. The child (and his mental states) is not seen for who he is, but in light of the parents' projections and distortions.
>
> . . .
>
> Some parents seem to have little notion of their baby's internal experience. These parents may simply seem oblivious to the fact that their child has feelings or thoughts that are particular and personal to him. When asked, for instance, about their child's reaction to separation, they reply "Nothing," or "Fine" . . . "He's cute," "He's pig-headed" . . . "She wakes up in the night screaming, screaming, but nothing really bothers her." (pp. 273, 278)

When feelings are routinely dismissed or minimized, when people are told things didn't happen—that personal experience tells them, did—when told they caused or wanted something, such as sexuality as a child—that personal experience tells them, they didn't—an environment like this has lasting consequences. It's maddening.

Even when interpersonal trauma occurs later on, in adulthood, we see the annihilation of intentionality. One client I worked with long ago, had suffered severe domestic violence to the point where she was a prisoner in her own home. True, she had plenty of chances to run away. Her husband would go to work, and she would wait for him in the apartment. This went on for months. She hid his threats and cruelty from friends and family and never went to the police. Why? Sure she was afraid, but beyond that, she'd lost her self-determination. The psychological imprisonment meant *she* was nowhere to be found. She'd lost herself in this disturbed relationship, living alongside some vague sense that he needed her, she needed him, she was *nothing* without him . . . what would she *do* with herself, anyway?

When trauma therapy goes well, over time people find in themselves greater intentionality, a renewed capacity for agency and self-determination. This fundamental human quality was something that, in Victor's case, had been lost for a time, something he rediscovered during our work together.

And although Victor came from a solid home background—his mother was one of his closest allies—intentionality was an important theme, especially in relation to the trauma. During the investigation and trial, it felt to him that everything was on autopilot, well out of his hands. All he wanted was to be normal, but he'd lost any say in his own life. Those in the community, upset by the collapse of the boys' choir, projected onto Victor and his family all kinds of malevolent intentions. They attributed the assault accusation to senseless spite. By some, Victor was labeled seductive: *the gay boy who wanted it.* None of this matched what he knew to be true about himself.

We worked on sorting that out. What, in fact, *was* his subjective experience? Originally, he *did* like Scott, yes, and he'd even found him attractive. But did he want to be *raped*? No.

And helping Victor reclaim intentionality was evident when it came to closely examining his feelings around Scott's request for forgiveness—what did *Victor* want, as opposed to what close others, like his father, expected of him? The therapy allowed Victor to make sense of his own wishes, what he imagined his future to look like, and his place in it. It was both freeing and growthful.

Reclaiming a Sense of Dignity

There are certain indignities that go along with interpersonal trauma. In the case of physical or sexual abuse, there's an invasion of body and private space. The person feels exposed, boundaries are crossed. In parental abandonment, there's the feeling of being unwanted or defective, unloved by those who should love us most. When there's betrayal, manipulation, or exploitation by close others, the person often feels naïve or foolish, humiliated: *How did I fall for that?*

Indignities like these wreak havoc on self-esteem. Indeed, when our dignity is taken, it robs us of personhood.

The client reclaims a sense of dignity, in part, through the therapeutic undertakings we've been looking at: when the person's experience is validated, when there's honesty in the interaction, when the therapist takes the suffering seriously—without judgment—when there's space to express vulnerable feelings, when conflicts in the therapeutic relationship are uncovered nondefensively, respectfully. When an approach like this is used, dignity can be reclaimed, slowly, in fits and starts.

But beyond anything the therapist says or does, or has much control over, clients also reclaim a sense of dignity by engaging *actively* in everyday life—when ready to do so, taking the risks that come with *doing*. Don't get me wrong, I've got nothing against reflection and understanding. Most of this book is about just that. But if some of what brings dignity is satisfaction in the ability to care for ourselves and others, pride in our work, a feeling of competence, then active engagement is a necessary ingredient.

Psychiatrist James Chu explained it well: "I am convinced that insights achieved in therapy are only the beginning, and the roots of self-esteem and a positive self-image are in actually *doing* things in life. Summoning up the courage to reach out and connect with others, going to work reliably, following through with an exercise program, and engaging in recreational activities are some examples" (2011, p. 118).

Work in a constructive environment can bring a sense of capability and autonomy. But like everything in mental health, there are few hard rules. And I've treated clients who, faced with alienation and harassment at work, gain little of value. They find retraumatization instead. And of course, we see this when people face a toxic home environment as well. In this situation, if they can allow themselves to leave, that can be the most dignified choice of all.

As people rediscover a sense of dignity, they develop new expectations of themselves and close others. Many realize they have abilities they'd previously overlooked. And when they make decisions for themselves—personal, forward-looking decisions—this may, at times, present new challenges for partners and friends.

When clients decide to change jobs, or go back to school, or become independent like never before, or show newfound confidence, this can be disorienting to close others. I saw this pattern in one of my clients, a grandmother who decided to return to college as a mature student, leaving her husband to run their small cannabis grow-op without her. As she spent more time studying for exams or writing essays, her frustrated husband complained about her never being around. But she was undeterred, completing the term with stellar grades. It was only after final exams that she realized her husband had put on about twenty-five pounds. Without her to keep him in check, he would smoke way too much weed. And when he smoked, he ate—a problem that concerned them both. Regardless, she signed up for the next semester (and got *him* to sign up for Weight Watchers).

My client discovered aspects of herself she wasn't aware of before: newfound confidence and interests, new awareness of her abilities; for example, that she was smart, that she could make good decisions for herself. In the time we worked together, I saw her make progress. She'd responded well to trauma therapy. But for her, going back to school also brought a feeling of pride, along with an enhanced view of herself.

It's very empowering for people when they reclaim a sense of dignity by engaging actively in everyday life—when they're ready—taking the risks that come with doing something different or something they value.

As I said above, when trauma therapy goes well, clients find new facets of themselves. And in the discovery, a measure of dignity is restored.

Reclaiming Values

Throughout the book, I've talked about the theme of deception. Trauma survivors are often deceived by others, and they deceive themselves—pretending things are normal when they aren't, cutting off painful feelings, putting a positive spin on dreadful experiences. When people live with the burden of self-deception, there's little room to express personal values, especially when their values differ from those of family and friends.

When good progress is made in trauma therapy, over time people find in themselves greater ability to access the values that matter to *them*. This often means clarifying what, in fact, their values are. The process can be illuminating, even exciting, for both therapist and client. With newfound opportunity to convey their values, the person may surprise themselves, putting forward ideas they'd rarely felt confident enough to voice.

In Chapter 6, I describe that for Victor the theme of *injustice* resonated personally: how unfair it felt to him that, because of the investigation and trial, and all that went with it, he and his family had lost so many friends. The trauma had dominated much of his adolescence, and in the end, they had to leave the community that they'd loved. To him, all of these represented injustices.

And he came to see the rape itself as unjust—as life sometimes can be. And while that perspective did make him sad, the conversation had shifted from what it was earlier on, when he was blaming himself for the rape and the fallout. At this point in treatment, Victor now expressed values he'd never before articulated, or hadn't seen as relevant to himself.

As I think about my relationship with Victor, it's easy for me to identify with him. If I'd been in his shoes, I'm confident *justice*—as a core value—would have resonated for me too. Throughout our work, my impression was that my values and his were well aligned.

But often that's not the case, nor should it be, necessarily. Sometimes therapist and client values are very different. In so many realms of our world— religion, education, child-rearing, sexuality, marriage—core conceptions of right and wrong vary widely. Ideas about what's important in life, what's moral, what we expect of others, and, of course, cultural differences are reflected in our values as well.

For one of my former students, differences in therapist-client values came across loud and clear. This supervisee (non-Jewish) was astonished by the enmeshment she saw in a Jewish family she was treating. She needed a quick reality check from me: *Just how often are Jewish men expected to call their mothers, anyway?* I assured her (based on personal experience): a lot.

My point? Our personal values and those of our clients are often at odds, especially if we differ culturally.

And when values do diverge, it's important that people be encouraged to speak for themselves. The client's expressed values should be *theirs*. In interpersonal trauma, manipulation from close others is so common. There's a risk the client will try to person-please, voicing the *therapist's* values, squelching their own.

As I've been saying, when treatment goes well, clients find new facets of themselves. Whenever I'm uncertain who people are actually speaking for, I ask: *Is that what you think? Or is that what I want to hear?* Self-determination is important in trauma therapy. Listening to our clients means listening to the values they claim for themselves.

A while back, my colleague psychologist Art Caspary gave me some very wise advice. We were discussing a challenging case, a woman I found frustrating to work with. Art put it well, when he said:

The "her" that you *want* her to be, isn't the "her" she imagines for herself.

Epilogue

I started this book quoting baseball pitcher and sexual abuse survivor R. A. Dickey. I'll end with the words of Mersiha Tufekčić.

Over the years, Mersiha has helped those who endured the war in Bosnia, which took place in the mid-1990s. Having lived through it herself, her commitment to trauma survivors was born of her own painful history, one she describes in a Canadian Broadcasting Corporation interview (Tremonti, 2013).

She was just eleven when the conflict started. Many children saw their parents killed by sniper fire. Mersiha and her family were forced to live in a concentration camp for two years. The conditions were those of extreme deprivation and abject poverty. Symptomatic well into adulthood, she described all she endured and how she recovered: the loss of childhood felt by so many, her recent experience with trauma therapy, and, ultimately, the tremendous impact that treatment had on her life.

Here are her words. And with these, we'll close:

> I work with [my therapist] for one year, more or less, and then I start to talk about my trauma. And since that moment, it was almost two years ago, I start to sleep finally. I stop trembling. I make progress. . . .
>
> You have to pass *through* the trauma, through the biggest pain, to continue normally with life.

References

Adamos, M. M. (2011). Is forgiveness a good thing? In G. Karabin & K. Wigura (Eds.), *Forgiveness: Promise, possibility and failure* (pp. 61–69). Oxford, UK: Inter-disciplinary Press.

Adichie, C. N. (2014). *Americanah*. New York, NY: Anchor Books, Random House.

Alexander, P. C. (2015). *Intergenerational cycles of trauma and violence: An attachment and family systems perspective*. New York, NY: Norton.

Allen, J. G., & Fonagy, P. (Eds.). (2006). *Handbook of mentalization-based treatment*. West Sussex, UK: Wiley.

Allen, J. G., Fonagy, P., & Bateman, A. W. (2008). *Mentalizing in clinical practice*. Arlington, VA: American Psychiatric Publishing.

Bakermans-Kranenburg, M. J., & van IJzendoorn, M. H. (2009). The first 10,000 adult attachment interviews: Distributions of adult attachment representations in clinical and nonclinical groups. *Attachment and Human Development, 11,* 223–263. doi:10.1080/14616730902814762.

Baranowsky, A. B., & Gentry, J. E. (2015). *Trauma practice: Tools for stabilization and recovery* (3rd ed.). Toronto, ON: Hogrefe.

Barbini, K. (Producer & Director), & Weinberg, S. (Co-Producer). (2010). *Boys and men healing from child sexual abuse* [Film]. San Diego, CA: Big Voice Pictures.

Basch, M. F. (1980). *Doing psychotherapy*. New York, NY: Basic Books.

Berger, A. M., Knutson, J. F., Mehm, J. G., & Perkins, K. A. (1988). The self-report of punitive childhood experiences of young adults and adolescents. *Child Abuse and Neglect, 12,* 251–262.

Berkowitz, B. (2015, March 5). The blue wall of silence among police enables cop brutality. *Buzzflash at Truthout.* Retrieved Dec. 4, 2017 from: http://www.truth-out.org/buzzflash/commentary/the-blue-wall-of-silence -among-police-enables-cop-brutality

Bick, K. (2011a, February 25). A corporal speaks: Ten questions for a Canadian who served in Afghanistan. *The Trauma and Mental Health Report.* Retrieved Dec. 4, 2017 from: http://trauma.blog.yorku.ca/2011/02/a-corporal-speaks-ten-questions-for-a-canadian-who-served-in-aghanistan/

Bick, K. (2011b, March 18). The view from here: Interview with a soldier's sister. *The Trauma and Mental Health Report.* Retrieved Dec. 4, 2017 from: http://trauma.blog.yorku.ca/2011/03/the-view-from-here-interview-with-a -soldiers-sister/

Bion, W. R. (1962). *Learning from experience.* London: Heinemann.

Björgvinsson T., & Hart, J. (2006). Cognitive behavioral therapy promotes mentalizing. In J. G. Allen, & P. Fonagy (Eds.), *Handbook of mentalization-based treatments* (pp. 157-170). Chichester, UK: Wiley.

Bohanek, J. G., Fivush, R., Zaman, W., Lepore, C. E., Merchant, S., & Duke, M. P. (2009). Narrative interaction in family dinnertime conversations. *Merrill-Palmer Quarterly, 55,* 488–515. doi:10.1353/mpq.0.0031.

Bowlby, J. (1980). *Attachment and loss: Vol. 3. Loss, sadness, and depression.* New York, NY: Basic Books.

Bowlby, J. (1988). *A secure base.* New York, NY: Basic Books.

Breuer, J., & Freud, S. (1955). Studies on hysteria. In J. Strachey (Ed. & Trans.), *Standard edition of the complete psychological works of Sigmund Freud* (Vol. 2, p. 6). London: Hogarth Press. (Original work published 1893–95)

Brooks, D. (2015, November 24). Tales of the super survivors. *The New York Times.* Retrieved Dec. 4, 2017 from: https://www.nytimes.com/2015/11/24/opinion/tales-of-the-super-survivors.html

Brooks, D. (2017, July 21). Republicans can't pass bills. *The New York Times.* Retrieved Dec. 4, 2017 from: https://www.nytimes.com/2017/07/21/opinion /republicans-bills-fail.html

Brown, B. (2012). *Daring Greatly.* New York, NY: Avery.

Burgess, A. W., Slattery, D. M., & Herlihy, P. A. (2013). Military sexual trauma: A silent syndrome. *Journal of Psychosocial Nursing, 51,* 20–26. doi:10.3928/02793695-20130109-03.

Burkeman, O. (2012). *The antidote: Happiness for people who can't stand positive thinking.* London: Penguin.

Calhoun, L. G., Cann, A., & Tedeschi, R. G. (2010). The posttraumatic growth model: Sociocultural considerations. In T. Weiss & R. Berger (Eds.), *Posttraumatic growth and culturally competent practice* (pp. 1–14). Hoboken, NJ: Wiley.

Calhoun, L. G., & Tedeschi, R. G. (1998). Posttraumatic growth: Future directions. In R. G. Tedeschi, C. L. Park, & L. G. Calhoun (Eds.), *Posttraumatic growth: Positive changes in the aftermath of crisis* (pp. 215–238). Mahwah, NJ: Erlbaum.

Carlat, D. J. (2004). *The psychiatric interview* (2nd ed.). New York, NY: Lippincott, Williams, & Wilkins.

Carter-Simmons, H. (2013, December 13). Family storytelling: Good for children (and parents). *The Trauma and Mental Health Report.* Retrieved Dec. 4, 2017 from: http://trauma.blog.yorku.ca/2013/12/family-storytelling-good-for-children-and-parents/

Chu, J. A. (2011). *Rebuilding shattered lives: Treating complex PTSD and dissociative disorders* (2nd ed.). Hoboken, NJ: Wiley.

Cinamon, J. S. (2016). *The relationship between parental support, parent emotional reaction, and parenting stress with children's posttraumatic stress symptoms following trauma-focused cognitive behavioral therapy* (Unpublished doctoral dissertation). York University, Toronto, ON.

Clark, C., Classen, C. C., Fourt, A., & Shetty, M. (2015). *Treating the trauma survivor: An essential guide to trauma-informed care.* New York, NY: Routledge.

Classen, C. C., Muller, R. T., Field, N. P., Clark, C., & Stern, E. M. (2017). A naturalistic study of a brief treatment program for survivors of complex trauma. *Journal of Trauma and Dissociation, 18,* 720–734. doi:10.1080/1529 9732.2017.1289492.

Classen, C. C., Zozella, K. P. M., Keating, L., Ross, D., & Muller, R. T. (2016, April). *Examining the interplay of attachment, alexithymia, and emotion regulation on trauma-related outcomes among women who completed a brief, intensive multi-modal program for adult survivors of child abuse.* Symposium presented at the 33rd annual conference of the International Society for the Study of Trauma and Dissociation, San Francisco, CA.

Cloitre, M., Cohen L. R., & Koenen, K. C. (2006). *Treating survivors of childhood abuse: Psychotherapy for the interrupted life*. New York, NY: Guilford Press.

Cloitre, M., Courtois, C. A., Charuvastra, A., Carapezza, R., Stolbach, B. C., & Green, B. L. (2011). Treatment of complex PTSD: Results of the ISTSS expert clinician survey on best practices. *Journal of Traumatic Stress, 24,* 615–627. doi:10.1002/jts.20697.

Cloitre, M., Courtois, C. A., Ford, J. D., Green, B. L., Alexander, P., Briere, J., . . . van der Hart, O. (2012). *The ISTSS expert consensus treatment guidelines for complex PTSD in adults*. Retrieved Dec. 4, 2017 from: https://www.istss.org/ISTSS_Main/media/Documents/ISTSS-Expert-Concesnsus-Guidelines-for-Complex-PTSD-Updated-060315.pdf

Cloitre, M., Stovall-McClough, K. C., Nooner, K., Zorbas, P., Cherry, S., Jackson, C. L., . . . Petkova, E. (2010). Treatment for PTSD related to childhood abuse: A randomized controlled trial. *American Journal of Psychiatry, 167,* 915–924.

Cohen, J. A., & Mannarino, A. P. (2005, October). *Treating traumatized children and their parents: Trauma-focused CBT for clinicians*. Invited workshop presented at the 2005 meeting of the Toronto Sexual Abuse Treatment Programs, Toronto, ON.

Cohen, J. A., Mannarino, A. P., & Deblinger, E. (2006). *Treating trauma and traumatic grief in children and adolescents*. New York, NY: Guilford Press.

Cordeiro, K., Foroughe, M., Muller, R. T., Bambrah, V., & Bint-Misbah, K. (2017, April). *Nonverbal behavioural coding of the Adult Attachment Interview*. Paper presented at the 34th annual conference of the International Society for the Study of Trauma and Dissociation, Washington, DC.

Cordeiro, K., Rependa, S. L., Muller, R. T., & Foroughe, M. F. (2018). EFFT and trauma: Engaging the parent with a dismissing attachment style. In M. F. Foroughe (Ed.), *Emotion focused family therapy with children and caregivers: A trauma-informed approach*. New York, NY: Routledge/Taylor and Francis.

Courtois, C. A. (2008). Complex trauma, complex reactions: Assessment and treatment. *Psychological Trauma: Theory, Research, Practice, and Policy, S*(1), 86–100. doi:10.1037/1942-9681.S.1.86.

Courtois, C. A., & Ford, J. D. (2013). *Treatment of complex trauma: A sequenced, relationship-based approach*. New York, NY: Guilford Press.

Dalenberg, C. J. (2000). *Countertransference and the treatment of trauma*. Washington, DC: American Psychological Association.

Diener, E., Colvin, C. R., Pavot, W. G., & Allman, A. (1991). The psychic cost of intense positive affect. *Journal of Personality and Social Psychology, 61*, 492–503.

Duarte Giles, M., Nelson, A. L., Shizgal, F., Stern, E. M., Fourt, A., Woods, . . . Classen, C. C. (2007). A multi-modal treatment program for childhood trauma recovery: Women Recovering from Abuse Program (WRAP). *Journal of Trauma and Dissociation, 8*, 7–24.

Ehrenreich, B. (2009). *Bright-sided: How the relentless promotion of positive thinking has undermined America*. New York, NY: Henry Holt.

Farber, B. (2015, June 25–July 1). Truth and genocide denial. *Now Magazine*, p. 17.

Fivush, R., & Sales, J. M. (2006). Coping, attachment, and mother-child narratives of stressful events. *Merrill-Palmer Quarterly, 52*, 125–150. doi:10.1353/mpq.2006.0003.

Fowles, S. M. (2013, March 28). The literary life of R. A. Dickey. *National Post*. Retrieved Dec. 4, 2017 from: http://nationalpost.com/afterword/the-literary-life-of-r-a-dickey

Frankfurt, H. G. (2005). *On bullshit*. Princeton, NJ: Princeton University Press.

Frewen, P., & Lanius, R. (2015). *Healing the traumatized self: Consciousness, neuroscience, treatment*. New York, NY: Norton.

Gaarder, E., & Belknap, J. (2002). Tenuous borders: Girls transferred to adult court. *Criminology, 40*, 481–518. doi:10.1111/j.1745-9125.2002.tb00964.x.

George, C., Kaplan, N., & Main, M. (1996). *Adult Attachment Interview* (3rd ed.). Unpublished manuscript, Department of Psychology, University of California, Berkeley.

Gilmore, S. (2015, January 22). Canada's race problem? It's even worse than America's. *Maclean's*. Retrieved Dec. 4, 2017 from: http://www.macleans.ca/news/canada/out-of-sight-out-of-mind-2/

Gobodo-Madikizela, P. (2004). *A human being died that night: A South African woman confronts the legacy of apartheid*. Boston: Houghton Mifflin Harcourt.

Godbout, N., Briere, J., Sabourin, S., & Lussier, Y. (2014). Child sexual abuse and subsequent relational and personal functioning: The role of parental support. *Child Abuse and Neglect, 38,* 317–325. doi:10.1016/j.chiabu.2013.10.001.

Goffman, E. (1971). *Relations in public: Microstudies of the public order.* New York, NY: Basic Books.

Gold, S. N. (2000). *Not trauma alone: Therapy for child abuse survivors in family and social contexts.* Philadelphia, PA: Taylor and Francis.

Goldberg, L. (2016, January 29). Rape survivors' fragmented memories misunderstood by media. *The Trauma and Mental Health Report.* Retrieved Dec. 4, 2017 from: http://trauma.blog.yorku.ca/2016/01/rape-survivors-fragmented-memories-misunderstood-by-media/

Herlihy, P. A., & Burgess, A. W. (2014). Breaking the silence of MST. *Journal of Employee Assistance,* 4th Quarter, 10–13. Retrieved Dec. 4, 2017 from http://hdl.handle.net/10713/4516.

Herman, J. L. (1992). *Trauma and recovery: The aftermath of violence from domestic abuse to political terror.* New York, NY: Basic Books.

Hesse, E. (1999). The Adult Attachment Interview: Historical and current perspectives. In J. Cassidy & P. R. Shaver (Eds.), *Handbook of attachment: Theory, research and clinical applications* (pp. 395–433). New York, NY: Guilford Press.

Hope, S., & Roslin, A. (2015). *Police wife: The secret epidemic of police domestic violence.* Golden Inkwell Books.

Hundt, N. E., & Holohan, D. R. (2012). The role of shame in distinguishing perpetrators of intimate partner violence in U.S. veterans. *Journal of Traumatic Stress, 25,* 191–197. doi:10.1002/jts21688.

Julien, D., & O'Connor, K. P. (2017). Recasting psychodynamics into a behavioral framework: A review of the theory of psychopathology, treatment efficacy, and process of change of the affect phobia model. *Journal of Contemporary Psychotherapy, 47,* 1–10. doi:10.1007/s10879-016-9324-9.

Junger, S. (2016). *Tribe: On homecoming and belonging.* Toronto, ON: HarperCollins.

Jurkovic, G. J. (1997). *Lost childhoods: The plight of the parentified child.* New York, NY: Brunner/Mazel.

Kashdan, T., & Biswas-Diener, R. (2014). *The upside of your dark side.* New York, NY: Penguin Random House.

Kaufman, G. (1992). *Shame: The power of caring* (3rd ed.). Rochester, VT: Schenkman Books.

Kelley, G., & Bloch, J. (Contributor). (2015, January 30). I'm sorry: The art and artifice of the apology [Radio program episode]. In G. Kelley (Executive Producer), *Ideas*. Toronto, ON: CBC Radio One.

Knoedel, S. (2009, November). *Military sexual trauma*. Paper presented at the Sexual Assault Prevention and Response Coordinator (SAPRC) annual training for the Wisconsin National Guard, Madison, WI.

Konanur, S., Muller, R. T., Cinamon, J. S., Thornback, K., & Zorzella, K. P. M. (2015). Effectiveness of trauma-focused cognitive behavioral therapy in a community-based program. *Child Abuse and Neglect, 50*, 159–170. doi:10.1016/j.chiabu.2015.07.013.

Labriola, T. (Producer). (1998). *Family therapy with the experts: Object relations therapy with Drs. Jill and David Scharff* [Video series]. Boston, MA: Allyn and Bacon.

Lemelson, R. (Producer & Director). (2009). *Forty years of silence: An Indonesian tragedy* [Film]. Los Angeles, CA: Elemental Productions.

Lewis, R. J., Griffin, J. L., Winstead, B. A., Morrow, J. A., & Schubert, C. P. (2003). Psychological characteristics of women who do or do not report a history of sexual abuse. *Journal of Prevention and Intervention in the Community, 26*, 49–65. doi:10.1300/J005v26n01_05.

Linehan, M. M. (1993). *Cognitive-behavioral treatment of borderline personality disorder*. New York, NY: Guilford Press.

Lithwick, D. (2009, January 10). Forgive not. *The New York Times*. Retrieved Dec. 4, 2017 from: http://www.nytimes.com/2009/01/11/opinion/11 lithwick.html

Lorinc, J. (2008, April 29). I solemnly promised to keep the secret. *The Globe and Mail*, p. F10.

Lukianoff, G., & Haidt, J. (2015, September). The coddling of the American mind. *The Atlantic*. Retrieved Dec. 4, 2017 from: https://www.theatlantic.com/magazine/archive/2015/09/the-coddling-of-the-american-mind/399356/

Manne, K. (2015, September 19). Why I use trigger warnings. *The New York Times*.

Marin, A. (2012, October). *In the line of duty: Investigation into how the Ontario Provincial Police and the Ministry of Community Safety and Correctional Services have addressed operational stress injuries affecting police officers*. Ombudsman Report, Ombudsman Ontario. Retrieved November 6, 2017, from https://www.ombudsman.on.ca/Files/sitemedia/Documents/Investigations/SORT%20Investigations/OPP-final-EN.pdf.

McCullough, L., & Andrews, S. (2001). Assimilative integration: Short-term dynamic psychotherapy for treating affect phobias. *Clinical Psychology: Science and Practice, 8,* 82–97.

Michaelson, J. (2015). *The gate of tears: Sadness and the spiritual path.* Teaneck, NJ: Ben Yehuda Press.

Minuchin, S. (1974). *Families and family therapy.* Cambridge, MA: Harvard University Press.

Minuchin, S. (2012). *Families and family therapy.* New York, NY: Routledge.

Minuchin, S., & Fishman, H. C. (1981). *Family therapy techniques.* Cambridge, MA: Harvard University Press.

Modell, A. H. (2009). Metaphor—the bridge between feelings and knowledge. *Psychoanalytic Inquiry, 29,* 6–11. doi:10.1080/07351690802246890.

Morris, D. J. (2015a, January 17). After PTSD, more trauma. *The New York Times.* Retrieved Dec. 4, 2017 from: https://opinionator.blogs.nytimes.com/2015/01/17/after-ptsd-more-trauma/

Morris, D. J. (2015b). *The evil hours: A biography of post-traumatic stress disorder.* Boston: Mariner Books.

Muller, R. T. (1993). *Shame and aggressive behavior in corporal punishment* (Unpublished doctoral dissertation). Michigan State University, East Lansing, MI. Retrieved Dec. 4, 2017 from: https://www.researchgate.net/publication/315379121_Shame_and_Aggressive_Behavior_in_Corporal_Punishment

Muller, R. T. (1995). The interaction of parent and child gender in physical child maltreatment. *Canadian Journal of Behavioural Science, 27,* 450–465.

Muller, R. T. (2001a). Child Abuse Shame Scale. Abstracted in J. Touliatos, B. F. Perlmutter, & G. W. Holden (Eds.), *Handbook of family measurement techniques* (Vol. 2, pp. 287–288). Thousand Oaks, CA: Sage.

Muller, R. T. (2001b). Child Abuse Shame Scale. In B. F. Perlmutter, J. Touliatos, & G. W. Holden (Eds.), *Handbook of family measurement techniques* (Vol. 3, p. 437). Thousand Oaks, CA: Sage.

Muller, R. T. (2009). Trauma and dismissing (avoidant) attachment: Intervention strategies in individual psychotherapy. *Psychotherapy: Theory, Research, Practice, Training, 46,* 68–81. doi:10.1037/a0015135.

Muller, R. T. (2010). *Trauma and the avoidant client: Attachment-based strategies for healing.* New York, NY: Norton.

Muller, R. T., Caldwell, R. A., & Hunter, J. E. (1993). Child provocativeness and gender as factors contributing to the blaming of victims of physical child abuse. *Child Abuse and Neglect, 17,* 249–260.

Muller, R. T., Caldwell, R. A., & Hunter, J. E. (1994). Factors predicting the blaming of victims of physical child abuse or rape. *Canadian Journal of Behavioural Science, 26,* 259–279.

Muller, R. T., Caldwell, R. A., & Hunter, J. E. (1995). The construct dimensionality of victim blame: The situations of physical child abuse and rape. *Personality and Individual Differences, 19,* 21–31.

Muller, R. T., & Hunter, J. E. (1995, October). *Factors predicting parental experience of shame over use of corporal punishment.* Paper presented at the 35th annual meeting of the New England Psychological Association, Wenham, MA.

Muller, R. T., Kraftcheck, E., & McLewin, L. A. (2004). Adult attachment and trauma. In D. R. Catherall (Ed.), *Handbook of Stress, Trauma, and the Family.* New York: Brunner-Routledge.

Muller, R. T., Lemieux, K., & Sicoli, L. A. (2001). Attachment and psychopathology among formerly maltreated adults. *Journal of Family Violence, 16,* 151–169.

Muller, R. T., & Rosenkranz, S. (2009). Attachment and treatment response among adults in inpatient treatment for Posttraumatic Stress Disorder. *Psychotherapy: Theory, Research, Practice, Training, 46,* 82-96.

Muller, R. T., Sicoli, L. A., & Lemieux, K. (2000). Relationship between attachment style and posttraumatic stress symptomatology among adults who report the experience of childhood abuse. *Journal of Traumatic Stress, 13,* 321–332.

Mytinger, M., & Madan, P. (Producers). (2010). *Ethan Watters: The globalization of the American psyche* [Videotaped interview]. Berkeley, CA: Berkeley Arts and Letters Programs. Retrieved Dec. 4, 2017 from http://library.fora.tv/2010/02/04/ Ethan_Watters_The_Globalization_of_the_American_Psyche

Najavits, L. M. (2002). *Seeking safety.* New York, NY: Guilford Press.

Noling, G. (2016, August 7). What the military owes rape survivors like my daughter. *The New York Times.* Retrieved Dec. 4, 2017 from: https:// www.nytimes.com/2016/08/09/opinion/what-the-military-owes-rape-survivors-like-my-daughter.html

Orwell, G. (1950). *1984.* New York, NY: Signet Classics.

Passarlay, G. (2016). *The lightless sky.* Toronto, ON: HarperCollins.

Paulson, D. S., & Krippner, S. (2007). *Haunted by combat: Understanding PTSD in war veterans.* New York, NY: Rowman and Littlefield.

Peale, N. V. (1994). *The power of positive thinking.* New York, NY: Random House. (Original work published 1952)

Perris, C. (2000). Personality-related disorders of interpersonal behaviour: A developmental-constructivist cognitive psychotherapy approach to treatment based on attachment theory. *Clinical Psychology and Psychotherapy, 7,* 97–117.

Presser, L. (2003). Remorse and neutralization among violent male offenders. *Justice Quarterly, 20,* 801–825. doi:10.1080/07418820300095701.

Rendon, J. (2015). *Upside: The new science of posttraumatic growth.* New York, NY: Touchstone.

Rependa, S., & Muller, R. T. (2015, April). *Therapeutic relationships and the traumatized child: Treatment alliance and symptomatology in child trauma using multi-rater perspectives.* Paper presented at the 32nd annual conference of the International Society for the Study of Trauma and Dissociation, Orlando, FL.

Rizvi, S. L., Steffel, L. M., & Carson-Wong, A. (2013). An overview of dialectical behavior therapy for professional psychologists. *Professional Psychology: Research and Practice, 44,* 73–80. doi:10.1037/a0029808.

Roslin, A. (2017). *Police wife: The secret epidemic of police domestic violence* (2nd ed.). Sugar Hill Books.

Said, E. (2005). Invention, memory, and place. In P. Leistyna (Ed.), *Cultural studies: From theory to action* (pp. 256–269). Oxford, UK: Blackwell.

Sapphire. (1996). *Push.* New York, NY: Vintage Books.

Shulevitz, J. (2015, March 21). In college and hiding from scary ideas. *The New York Times.* Retrieved Dec. 4, 2017 from: https://www.nytimes.com/2015/03/22/opinion/sunday/judith-shulevitz-hiding-from-scary-ideas.html?mtrref=www.google.ca&assetType=opinion

Simpson, J. (2015, June 2). Fixating on the past makes progress difficult. *The Globe and Mail.* Retrieved Dec. 4, 2017 from: https://www.theglobeandmail.com/opinion/fixating-on-the-past-makes-progress-difficult/article24759214/

Slade, A. (2004). Two therapies: Attachment organization and the clinical process. In L. Atkinson & S. Goldberg (Eds.), *Attachment issues in psychopathology and intervention* (pp. 181–206). Mahwah, NJ: Erlbaum.

Slade, A. (2005). Parental reflective functioning: An introduction. *Attachment and Human Development, 7,* 269–281. doi:10.1080/14616730500245906.

Smith, M. L., & Glass, G. V. (1977). Meta-analysis of psychotherapy outcome studies. *American Psychologist, 32,* 752–760.

Smith, M. L., Glass, G. V., & Miller, T. I. (1980). *The benefits of psychotherapy.* Baltimore, MD: Johns Hopkins University Press.

Sopher, R. (2015, July 21). Our secret Auschwitz. *The New York Times.* Retrieved Dec. 4, 2017 from: https://opinionator.blogs.nytimes.com/2015/07/21/our-secret-auschwitz/

Steele, H., & Steele, M. (Eds.). (2008). *Clinical applications of the Adult Attachment Interview.* New York, NY: Guilford Press.

Stovall-McClough, K. C., & Cloitre, M. (2006). Unresolved attachment, PTSD, and dissociation in women with childhood abuse histories. *Journal of Consulting and Clinical Psychology, 74,* 219–228. doi:10.1037/0022-006X.74.2.219.

Talaga, T. (2016, December 14). St. Anne's residential school survivors must wait longer for justice. *The Toronto Star.* Retrieved Dec. 4, 2017 from https://www.thestar.com/news/canada/2016/12/14/st-annes-residential-school-survivors-must-wait-longer-for-justice.html

Taylor, C. (2008, February 16). One million tiny plays about Britain. *The Guardian.* Retrieved Dec. 4, 2017 from: https://www.theguardian.com/lifeandstyle/2008/feb/16/familyandrelationships1

Tremonti, A. M. (Host). (2013, March 4). Bosnia special [Radio program episode]. In K. Goldhar (Executive Producer), *The Current.* Toronto, ON: CBC Radio One.

van der Hart, O., Brown, P., & van der Kolk, B. A. (1989). Pierre Janet's treatment of post-traumatic stress. *Journal of Traumatic Stress, 2,* 379–395.

Viorst, J. (1986). *Necessary losses.* New York, NY: Free Press.

Wallin, D. J. (2007). *Attachment in psychotherapy.* New York, NY: Guilford Press.

Wampold, B. E. (2001). *The great psychotherapy debate: Models, methods, and findings.* Mahwah, NJ: Erlbaum.

Watters, E. (2010). *Crazy like us: The globalization of the American psyche.* New York, NY: Free Press.

Weisman, R. (2014). *Showing remorse: Law and the social control of emotion.* Burlington, VT: Ashgate.

White, M., & Epston, D. (1990). *Narrative means to therapeutic ends*. New York, NY: Norton.

Zorzella, K. P. M., Muller, R. T., & Cribbie, R. A. (2015). The relationships between therapeutic alliance and internalizing and externalizing symptoms in trauma-focused cognitive behavioral therapy. *Child Abuse and Neglect, 50*, 171–181. doi:10.1016/j.chiabu.2015.08.002.

Zorzella, K. P. M., Rependa, S. L., & Muller, R. T. (2017). Therapeutic alliance over the course of child trauma therapy from three different perspectives. *Child Abuse and Neglect, 67*, 147–156. doi:10.1016/j.chiabu.2017.02.0320145-2134.

Index